From one horse
lover to another
Shelley Riley

Casual Lies

A Triple Crown Adventure

Shelley Riley

—

DEDICATED TO THE MEMORY of Jim Riley, my mother, Helen Eisemann, my father, Larry Eisemann (for sacrificing so much to buy me my first horse), Casual Lies, and of course, lest I forget, good old Brownie. My life was made better for having known and loved them all. My memories would be a bleak landscape without the color and life they added.

Contents

Acknowledgments

I WANT TO THANK Tracy Gantz-White and Don Walters, both editors with first-hand horse racing experience. Their knowledge and endless patience proved a priceless commodity while working on this memoir.

My thanks to Paula Chinick, who convinced me I should change a bag full of notes written on used envelopes, empty bags and three ring binder paper into a book that brought all the love and wonder of Casual Lies back into crisp focus for me.

Heartfelt thanks go out to my non-horsey friends Jane Miceli, Jeanette Faenzi, Marilyn Morse, Pam Copeland and Sharon Tietgens, whom I abused endlessly, making them endure re-writes for clarity.

Sheryl Sheaffer, a very accomplished beta reader, my appreciation for her valuable insight.

Finally my gratitude to Benoit Photo of Arcadia California for allowing me to reproduce their amazing photos for this book.

Preface

Over the years, my fantasy as a trainer of Thoroughbreds involved winning any one of three races—the Hollywood Futurity, Hollywood Gold Cup or the Washington, D. C., International.

"What, no Kentucky Derby?" you ask.

It wasn't that I didn't love the Kentucky Derby. Every year on the first Saturday in May, my husband Jim, and I would rush through our chores so we could be home, feet up, when the first strains of "My Old Kentucky Home" came over the television. Tears would come to my eyes while I watched the magnificent horses taking their first steps onto the track. The grandstand seemed filled to bursting as the horses paraded for the fans, the famed twin spires towering above them. I was always entranced by the spectacle that is the Kentucky Derby, but I'd never remotely considered the possibility of one day being a trainer who would saddle a horse with a chance of winning this historic race.

I suppose it was the Kentucky Derby's sheer magnitude. As one of the most famous races in the world, Kentucky's Run for the Roses seemed so unattainable that I could more easily imagine finding a 10-carat diamond in the birdfeeder than ever competing in it.

And yet, here I stood next to Jim, heart pounding as I watched my wonderful Casual Lies approach the starting gate at Churchill Downs. Once loaded, the gate banged open and the field was away in the 118th running of the

Kentucky Derby. The roar of more than 137,000 racing fans intensified the excitement, anxiety and apprehension that was making it so hard for me to catch my breath. I was now less than two minutes away from untold joy or grinding disappointment.

Chapter One

Within Reach

"Sold! To the lady in the sixth row for $7,500." So it began—the small, brown, nondescript colt destined to change my life forever was now mine.

I had a lot to learn before I gambled my future on that life-changing bid at a mixed bloodstock sale in Lexington, Kentucky, on a snowy January day in 1990.

When I chose to follow a career training racehorses, a profession historically dominated by men, I understood it would take years to develop skills that would make me competitive.

My love of horses and borderline obsession with them were my greatest strengths, while an unflagging optimism gave me the mindset for dealing with the capricious nature of these beautiful and volatile animals. Still, my passion alone would not bring long-term success; that would need to be earned through the experience gained from handling as many horses as possible.

I can pinpoint with a certain amount of accuracy the moment I first discovered my fascination with horses. I was six years old, and I wasn't dragging my little red wagon around thinking about running a horse in the Kentucky Derby. I was dragging it through a field of giant sunflowers behind our house in California as I collected caterpillars.

The adventure was the allure on the day the enormous sunflowers turned into an imaginary forest of magical green and gold trees. They towered high above, sheltering me from the sun as I went about collecting my fuzzy prizes. Suddenly I was startled by the sound of jangling metal and the thud of heavy feet. I looked up, amazed by the sight of a huge black horse pushing his way through the forest, pulling a plow.

There I stood, caught red-handed with the stolen caterpillars in my wagon. I stared at the magnificent horse looming high above me, his nostrils flaring as he sniffed the top of my head. Holding the reins, the farmer watched me reach up tentatively to pat the bewhiskered, rubbery lips of the massive draft horse.

The old farmer asked if I would like to ride the horse. I was filled with wonder as he lifted me up over his head and I found myself astride Blackie's broad back, the smell of sweaty horse overwhelming my senses. With a flick of the reins, Blackie took his first lumbering step forward, and I was hooked for life.

I had collected my last caterpillar; instead I searched the plowed rows every day, looking for Blackie to ride while he worked in the fields. Astride my glorious mount, my imagination was set free. I was a fairy princess surveying my kingdom of golden flowers.

Many years passed, and with an unending barrage of begging and pestering, my dad finally bought my first horse for $250. There wasn't a fancy stable, no riding lessons; Dad rented a paddock at an old defunct farm not far from Moffett Field in Mountain View and only a few miles from where we lived. My father made it my responsibility to care for my horse before and after school, every day, rain or shine.

Located close to the trails that snaked around the San Francisco Bay, the place where I rode my very own horse was quiet and lonely. With the sea breezes blowing in my face, I taught myself to ride and eventually raced around on Honey like a mad thing.

Gaining confidence in my riding skills, I competed in events from time to time. I tried gymkhana, team roping and got my head cracked open in an attempt to be the first female bull rider in our area. The bull-riding career lasted three jumps out of the chute. When I regained consciousness, flat on my back on the arena floor, I'd been rewarded with a thorough dirt bath, concussion, deep scalp laceration and a mouth full of green bull stuff. Looking back, I think it was only the green bull stuff that really kept me from trying it again.

A few years later I was working for a radiologist during the week, while cleaning stalls for free on the weekends at the Bay Meadows spring Quarter Horse meet. I didn't need to be paid. I looked upon it as an apprenticeship that would help me learn, first hand, about the beautiful racehorses. My imagination was flirting with the idea that someday I would be training horses just like these.

This is where I met Jim Riley. He was a lifelong horseman and a skilled jockey. It wasn't love at first sight. A few inches shorter than I was and a man of few words, he would say little or nothing as I legged him up on the horses. Short or not, for my part I blushed every time he looked at me. Fate chose us to be a team, and when the race meet ended, we were in love, married and on our way to Los Alamitos, the next stop in the Quarter Horse racing season.

~

JIM'S FATHER HAD PUT HIM astride his first horse when he was little more than a toddler. Over the years Jim sharpened his skills by breaking horses, working on cattle ranches and riding broncs and bulls on the rodeo circuit. He guided dudes back into the wilderness on hunting trips and even broke horses for the movies—big, strong five-year-olds that had never been touched by human hands. He spent many years galloping horses, both on training farms and at the racetrack, before he got his jockey's license and started riding races at Los Alamitos, Bay Meadows and the California fair circuit. Jim had magic in his hands, and when he started the breaking process from scratch, the horses ended up well mannered and focused on running.

Jim and I raced mainly in Northern California during the late 1970s, when I started my racing stable. The day I saddled my first horse as a fledgling trainer, Jim guided her to an easy win at the Sonoma County Fair in Santa Rosa.

In the beginning, I mostly trained Quarter Horses and only the occasional Thoroughbred. But since the money and the glory were with the Thoroughbreds, I began to focus my attention in that direction. Slowly the ratio of Quarter Horses to Thoroughbreds shifted to where I rarely had a Quarter Horse in the barn unless it belonged to me.

My first forays into buying racing prospects took place in Northern California. I bought those horses cheap, and I ran them where they belonged. I still wasn't having fantasies of the Run for the Roses; my aspiration was to find a horse with outstanding potential and win races. In some ways it was comparable to playing the slot machines in Vegas; would one more dollar in the next machine be the one to provide the jackpot? You would never know unless you tried.

Operating a full-service training business, breaking colts, conditioning horses to race and running at all the major meets eventually expanded into pinhooking—that is, buying a young horse to resell at a profit the following year.

I knew early on, the only way I was going to get an exceptionally good horse in my barn and run it under my name would be if I found it myself. If I happened upon a horse that turned out to be something above the average, my choice would then be to sell it at a horses-in-training sale or keep it and race it as my own. Either way would help build my reputation as a racehorse trainer and not just someone who solely specialized in breaking young thoroughbreds for other trainers, sending them on well-behaved, conditioned and nearly ready to run.

Eventually, Kentucky beckoned because that's arguably where some of the best horses in the world were concentrated. Jim and I had never been to Kentucky, however, so we had to make the decision to broaden our horizons and look beyond our safe and familiar California-based sales.

If you've never been to the bloodstock sales in Lexington, Kentucky, you've missed the Mall of America, horsemen's style. Despite the obvious similarities with sales in California, the scope is at an entirely different level. Kentucky is a genuine cornucopia of horses—we could literally sift through thousands of young prospects rather than the dozens we were accustomed to in our home state.

In 1987, the horse market had plunged into bad times. Ever optimistic, I hoped we had found the right time to pluck a ripe plum while helpless breeders were still licking their wounds. We withdrew from our savings account what we thought we could afford to lose—$10,000 in cashier's checks—and headed to the Keeneland September yearling sale.

As we left Lexington's Blue Grass Airport in our rental car, we found we couldn't stop smiling. Every direction we turned we saw rolling, white-fenced pastures grander than entire farms in California. Bands of horses, their coats gleaming in the sun, strolled about, heads down munching on this vast carpet of green. We had left California in the morning and arrived at horse heaven in the afternoon. What horseman could ask for anything more? We must have looked like two five-year-olds crossing the threshold of Toys R Us.

Jim and I brought with us boundless enthusiasm. We had come, we would look, we would see and most assuredly we would conquer. The sale had five thick catalogs full of horses—how could we possibly fail to find a runner with so many to choose from?

Keeneland Association sits in a breathtakingly beautiful park-like setting off Versailles Road, just across the road from the airport. The grounds contain a racecourse as well as one of the finest Thoroughbred sales facilities in the world. Once you pass through the impressive stone entry, the long lane leads to a parking area that more closely resembles a tree farm than a parking lot. Row upon row of pin oaks spread their canopies overhead. Beams of sunlight pierce the leafy umbrella, adding a subtle charm to the surroundings.

Passing the racetrack en route to the sales facility, we paused to admire the grandstand, a classic limestone structure with graceful arches, clinging ivy runners, hunter green trim and a bounty of colorful flowering shrubs. I could only imagine what it would be like to saddle a horse in the understated elegance of the saddling paddock, located at the far end of the grandstand and sheltered by huge oak trees.

The sales pavilion nestles right into this grand setting, and the heart of this building is where the auctioning of the horses takes place. The auction floor has reserved theater-type seating along with a dais where each yearling is showcased while the bidding is under way.

The real action, however, happens behind the two rolling doors at the rear of the dais. A divided pit, chute and huge covered circular walk ring are all abuzz with activity as buyers try to discover a star on parade. Each horse in the walk ring is led across the chute to the pit, where they wait prior to entering the sales ring. Two bid spotters stand in raised cubicles on each side of the pit, and while other bid spotters are located in the pavilion, these two fetch the majority of the winning bids.

Every one of these areas holds danger for prospective bidders. Standing in the designated observation areas would seem prudent and safe. Unfortunately, people who bid on untried yearlings are not necessarily prudent or overly concerned about safety. You can be watching a colt acting up on the other side of the ring, "safe" behind the railing, when suddenly a hind hoof whizzes past your head. Countless times I have seen a yearling narrowly miss mowing down someone as the young horse stampedes around the middle of the walk ring at the end of a lead shank.

The chute and pit pose the most danger. The chute leading to the pit is also the walkway to get from one side of the pavilion to the other. Handlers try to lead fractious yearlings through crowds of people intent on their own agenda while the voice of the auctioneer blasts away on loudspeakers. The majority of the crowd tends to talk at the top of their lungs in an attempt to be heard over the bedlam. Punctuating this chaos are the frequent boom and thunk as a hoof connects with wood.

Horses are whinnying excitedly, eyes rolling, nostrils flared. Some dance around, teetering on the edge of control, kicking, rearing and striking. Other yearlings stand quietly, seemingly unperturbed by the cacophony of noise and excitement. I like the yearlings that are alert but controlled, curious while apparently enjoying the whole process. This goes on from 10:00 in the morning to 9:00 in the evening or later, horse after horse, without a break, day after day, until the last horse is sold.

Jim and I headed to the relative calm and tranquility of the barn area first, eager to see the yearlings we had picked out of the catalog to inspect. Because the stable area was so vast and spread out, a shuttle service ferried prospective buyers between the various barns and the sales pavilion. Everywhere you looked, gorgeous horses paraded to their best advantage under the gigantic old oaks between every barn—minus dust and flies. How did they do that? I could understand the no-dust part—it was the no-flies part that was truly amazing.

A bit overwhelmed at first with the sale's sheer magnitude, we just watched as others examined horses. We saw no sense lusting after horses whose siblings had won a multitude of top-class, prestigious races when our budget only extended to $10,000.

The number one rule for shopping at the yearling sales is to know your equine conformation like an artist knows anatomy. Secondly, since most horses have faults, you need to know which conformation faults will most likely cause problems when you start serious training.

The majority of buyers who attend the sales have a good eye for a horse. If you doubt that, just watch as one of the nicer prospects is headed toward the sales pavilion. You'd better be prepared to move fast, lest you get trampled underfoot by the human herd hot on its heels.

On that very first day at Keeneland, we spotted a gray filly that simply took our breath away. She was athletic, correct, poised and lovely—we stood there mesmerized. It was the horse of our dreams. We would gladly spend our entire bankroll on her alone.

Calculations flew. After Jim and I projected our future income to see how much we could exceed our original $10,000 for purchasing a horse, we were ready to make a winning bid on this pretty filly. She was selling late in the sale, and as we watched, many horses went by—brown, bay, tall, short, fat, lean, docile, on the muscle. We looked, we watched, but we could not be tempted. We had seen our goal and she was gray.

When at long last she arrived in the holding area, we were still hopeful that with any luck she might get overlooked. Although she had a good pedigree, the filly was in fact out of a young unproven mare, and there was nothing special about the runners in the previous generation of the mare's family either.

As she entered the walk ring, appearing both confident and poised, she seemed to be attracting a lot of attention. She really did look like a runner. Once she entered the pit, she was only two numbers away from going under the hammer. The crowd enveloped her, blocking our view. Huddled as close as we could get, the sales pavilion seemed as busy and congested as Grand Central Station during rush hour.

The fantasy of owning this filly clarified with each breath I took. The only thing I hadn't done was give her a name. The door rolled open, and the last we saw of our dream-come-true was her nearly white rump as it sashayed through the portal of the sales ring, disappearing from view.

My heart pounded with anxiety—I could hardly swallow. They finished the introduction, and the auctioneer said, "Who would like to open this good-looking filly at fifty?" FIFTY!!! Oh no, he couldn't mean five, zero, zero, zero, zero. Astonished, I turned to meet Jim's gaze. In less than three minutes, "Sold, $240,000" rang throughout the pavilion.

How did we feel? Not stunned. Stunned was at $50,000. Not deflated. It was too early for that. As Jim and I crept away, eyes downcast, with our $10,000 in cashier's checks tucked safely out of sight, the word "foolish" definitely came to mind. Obviously, management designated the first two days of the sale as "select yearlings" for good reason. An athletic filly wasn't going to go unnoticed no matter how light the family tree.

We comforted ourselves in knowing we had good taste selecting the gray filly—and were thankful we hadn't been tempted to bid far more than we could afford. We cowered out of the traffic lane, discussing where we had gone wrong. Down but not beaten, we picked ourselves up and ventured forth, ready to try again. After all, there were plenty more where she came from, another four catalogs full to be exact. The horses to be auctioned off continued coming down the lane, seemingly without end.

As the day wore on into the early evening, the ache in our feet had spread upward, joint by joint, to settle between our shoulder blades. The horses hadn't just begun to look alike. They all looked like more money than we had to spend, more than everything we owned put together—house, car, savings, future earnings. What were we doing here?

~

TRUDGING THROUGH A SECOND day of sales, dehydrated from the heat and thoroughly discouraged, we crept into the nearly empty air-conditioned pavilion with its reserved seating. We felt we would be relatively safe from immediate eviction, having found what we hoped was a discreet pair of cushioned chairs toward the back.

I convinced myself I could see everything I needed to see about each and every horse from my borrowed seating. I was about to acknowledge the specter of defeat when suddenly a huge chestnut colt strode into the ring. He looked more like a two-year-old than a yearling.

When the bidding began, it climbed very slowly. What's the matter, $3,500? I looked around. Everybody must have gone to the bathroom. We had passed the bars on the way in, and they overflowed with the day's thirsty bidders. The bid crept up to $4,000. Was this what I had come for, the moment I had waited for, the opportunity?

The colt's sire, His Majesty, was a bit old, but a good horse. The youngster's front legs looked correct—what's wrong?

"Forty-two hundred, are you through?" the auctioneer called. "We're going to sell him. Going once, going twice, $4,500—SOLD."

Jim sat up, electrified. "What did you do?"

"Why, I just bought that horse," I said, maybe a teensy bit breathless, heart still pounding.

"He's huge. He's a moose!" Jim replied, thunderstruck.

"Oh, he wasn't that big."

"Shelley, trust me, it was pure luck he fit through the door."

As we left the pavilion to take a look at our new purchase, I overheard two men talking.

"Did you see that red colt that just sold? They had to raise the air-conditioners to get him in the building."

Loud laughter echoed in our ears. Jim snorted and shook his head.

We drove away more realistic, smarter for the experience and, as it turned out, with a lot more than we had bargained for. Unfortunately, we had still a harder lesson yet to learn about swimming in the big boys' pool.

When our purchase arrived in California a week later with his leg joints swelling unnaturally, we were taken aback. X-rays showed that these swellings were not likely injuries sustained on the van en route. Our huge His Majesty colt showed indications of a hereditary condition developing in a joint in one of his back legs—not a good thing, since a horse runs by driving off his hind end. Unfortunately, he never amounted to much as a racehorse.

~

A COUPLE OF YEARS LATER, taking the opportunity to reduce the interest rate on our home mortgage, we refinanced our house. I discussed it with Jim, and we decided to take out some equity. Buying yearlings with borrowed money? At first glance, that might not seem such a good idea. As an investment in our pinhooking business, we considered it an opportunity to buy a higher quality of horse, thereby bettering our prospects for success.

I had several successful buying trips under my belt by the time I decided to give the January 1990 Keeneland mixed sale a go. The foals at this sale were technically yearlings, since all Thoroughbreds turn a year older on January 1, but in reality they were still babies, ranging in age from approximately five to 11 months.

You have to have a different mindset when looking at what are termed "short" yearlings. You must look past the gawkiness and ignore the inherent cute factor while trying to imagine the horse he or she will become. You'll pay less in January, but you are going to take bigger risks than if you waited for the fall venues to buy your prospects.

At home during this time of year, we were getting horses ready for sale dates and race dates, so Jim stayed in California to oversee those operations as I traveled to Kentucky. At the sale on my own this time, I completed my crack-of-dawn tour of the barns, hustling through falling snow to arrive at the sales pavilion ahead of my first pick of the day. All the required players were in place when I arrived—grooms, bid spotters, auctioneers, horses. Where were the bidders? I saw maybe five other people. Perhaps they were having coffee and donuts or maybe were tucked away cozy and warm in the reserved seating area.

At any rate, the lack of competition would certainly make it easier to do my job. I sidled up to the pit and dug around in my dog-eared catalog as they announced the day's updates. I made it a habit to write them all down, just in case.

As I leaned on the rail of the pit, the catalog open in my hands, my glance settled on the colt standing in front of me. At the exact moment my eyes focused on the colt's head, he turned toward me and made direct eye contact.

I still catch my breath today when I remember the intensity of my reaction to him. This colt wasn't looking at the surroundings. He was looking at me—and his eyes sparkled so quizzically! I can't tell you how many times people have asked me how I found Casual Lies, but truly, in retrospect, I think it's more likely he may have found me.

I have often thought of that moment when I huddled close to the overhead heaters, trying to get warm on a freezing morning, completely engrossed in the pages of my catalog. Something made me look at the head of this tiny, weedy, fuzzy, dull-coated, nondescript colt, and *something* made him look at me with his bright-eyed gaze in an electrifying experience.

I have contemplated all the circumstances, all the choices that I had made along the way. What if I had arrived five minutes later? What if I had walked up to the other pit to lean on the rail? What if I had headed into the pavilion to get a cup of coffee? All the things that had to happen *did* happen to put me there, alone at the rail, at that exact moment in time, the moment when I needed to see one particular colt as he turned his head and two destinies came together, equine and human.

When I finally broke eye contact, I looked him over quickly. I didn't have much time; he was two numbers away. I went into the pit and checked his conformation—front, back, both sides—and the whole time he tried to nuzzle and nibble my fingers, curious and mischievous. That beautiful head, those big eyes. . . if I was going to bid on him, I had to drag myself away.

With a dry, dead-looking coat, he wasn't eye-catching, but he was a well-bred son of the stallion Lear Fan, balanced and possessing a presence that was readily apparent once you really looked. He was definitely the type who might slip through the cracks.

The catalog updates I had written down earlier indicated he had a full sister who'd just run extremely well in a prestigious race in New York, literally days before he was due to go under the hammer. This was a pinhooker's dream come true because with a sister actively running well, she could improve his resale chances in another year—truly the perfect position for a buyer to be in.

A very good and admired friend of mine, Dr. Jack Woolsey, described it best when he said: I stood like a hawk on a wire prepared to swoop when the opportunity arose. In fact, I was about to hit the mega jackpot.

I recall that my hands shook slightly as I signed the $7,500 sales slip for my new Lear Fan colt on that wintry day. Although less starry-eyed, naïve and wet behind the ears than I'd been on previous sales trips to Kentucky, I was still excited and optimistic that I could find a runner. I just had to be persistent and, oh yes, lest we forget, get lucky.

Unfortunately, buyer's remorse was building up a head of steam as doubts began to assail me. After all, I would be paying for this colt with borrowed money.

I felt the colt had gone way too cheaply. Considering the strength of his catalog page with the impressive update, if somebody important wanted him, they would have been there. That naturally led to thoughts of a problem I may have overlooked. With my hurried inspection of him in the confines of the pit, could I have missed something? If that was indeed the case, could such a problem compromise his chances of ever running competitively?

I felt compelled to check more thoroughly and headed like a bullet to the barn where the colt was stabled. Paying scant attention to the beauty of the barn area covered in snow, I contemplated how the bidding had gone. Usually I didn't start bidding on horses until after they had passed at least the $5,000 mark. I had found, in general, if they were still going up $500 or $1,000 per bid, they were more likely to stay within my top range.

Adrenaline still pumping, I reflected on the moment when the tiny Lear Fan colt went into the ring. I had hurried from the pit area and positioned myself inside, sitting near one of the bid spotters. When the bidding started, no one seemed willing to make an opening bid at any price.

As the auctioneer kept dropping the bid and there still wasn't any interest, I became worried. At the point when "Are you finished?" rang out, I jumped in with a $2,500 bid. It was totally out of character for me to be the opening bid, but I really wanted this colt and I didn't want the hammer to come down without having made a single offer.

Ultimately, I was one of only two bidders. The other bidder sat three rows up on the left and was topping my bids $500 at a time. Being first in on the bidding puts you on the defensive rather than the offensive, forcing you into the position of defending your claim at each bid. I was prepared to take the bid to $20,000, which, of course, the other bidder didn't know, but I certainly wanted to pay as little as possible.

Still, I was relieved that the bidding had surged past my magic $5,000 mark. When you're pinhooking, prospective buyers of two-year-olds show a decided lack of respect for yearlings purchased for less than $5,000. Sometimes they won't even bother to look at all.

As the other bidder and I continued our $500 dance to the $6,000 level, I knew I needed to take the offense. So I punched the bid up $1,500 to test his resolve. This would put me on the offensive and I would find out how serious this guy was going to be past $6,000. Was he bidding me up or did he really want this colt? Evidently, he wasn't very serious and dropped out after I took the lead. You have to wonder if this fellow ever followed up and found out he was the underbidder on Casual Lies.

In the horse racing business, $7,500 is a pittance. Keep in mind, raising your hand at auction is the easy part. If you plan to race this horse, when the hammer falls, you just signed up for a minimum two-year commitment. The responsibility for the welfare of this animal is now squarely in your lap. It's a very expensive commitment—shipping, boarding, feed, veterinarian, shoeing, dentistry, insurance, nomination fees—and all that before he ever runs his first race. Furthermore, no dollar figure can be put on the emotional commitment. What price can you put on a dream, hoping the dream will come true?

Beneath the spreading branches of the gigantic oak trees, my new purchase appeared weedier, hairier and even smaller as he stood in the swirling snowflakes. I had also missed a very slight toeing out on the right hind foot. Nonetheless, try as I might, I still couldn't find anything glaringly wrong with the colt. He would grow and fill out, that was a given. Would he grow the way I wanted?

I immediately discovered that this colt's strong suit was personality. If he wasn't trying to get my fingers in his mouth, it was my coat sleeve or the catalog. I had to close the snaps he'd opened on my coat several times. He was curious and friendly, and I was thoroughly charmed.

I called Jim in California. He was just finishing up at the barn. I told him I had managed to make my first purchase and shared the hip number with him. Over the background sounds of our busy shedrow, I could hear Jim leafing through the catalog, then the pause as he looked over the colt's page.

The first words I heard were, "What's wrong with him?"

I had a fairly good idea what must be going through Jim's mind. He would know that we could not likely afford the colt described on this catalog page unless he had some serious conformation flaws. I told Jim that the colt toed out a little on the right hind, but other than that he was fairly correct.

"Better back than front. What did you have to give for him?"

"Seventy-five hundred."

"Jeez, you're kidding. What does he look like?"

"Well. . .he's brown," I replied hesitantly. After all, given his small stature and scruffy coat, I couldn't exactly wax eloquent about what a great-looking individual he was.

"Yes?"

"Well, he's hairy," I added.

"And?"

"And nothing," I shot back, somewhat defensively. "He's small and he's not very thrifty. He'll grow. He's a late May foal."

We get no guarantees when it comes to buying a runner, and nobody knew it better than Jim. But Jim definitely trusted my eye and my judgment, and he was satisfied and excited to have such a well-bred colt in our lineup.

As for me, I began to imagine how exciting it would be to arrive at our barn just as the sun begins to brighten the sky. Waiting to greet us—well within reach—would be a new face, a new challenge and our brand new bright-eyed opportunity eagerly awaiting his first tub of oats.

Chapter Two

Nothing Comes Easy

Once paid for at the cashier's office, my new Lear Fan yearling was loaded on a van and headed for California. Leaving the snow-covered Kentucky bluegrass behind, he would travel cross-country to his new home in California's sunny San Joaquin Valley: final destination, Visalia and Darlene Shoemaker's Two Ton Tony Farm. It was my hope that the tiny colt would flourish in the warmer central California weather.

As a pinhooker, I planned to sell Casual Lies at the March 1991 Barretts two-year-old-in-training sale in Pomona, California, although admittedly this was a very early sale date for a very late May foal. To make a good showing at the Barretts sale, my little Raggedy Andy would need to make remarkable physical changes over the next eight months before we started to break him to saddle and teach him his early lessons.

A very professional horsewoman with years of experience in all aspects of Thoroughbred husbandry, Darlene soon discovered Casual Lies was suffering from chronic foal pneumonia, and for that reason he was isolated from other yearlings on the farm. Along with the pneumonia, Darlene reported that the poor little guy had stepped off the van with all four legs swollen from hoof to knee, a puffy inflammation that could have been attributed to the extended road trip.

Although the puffiness receded over the next few days, a severe case of epiphysitis remained. Basically an inflammation of the growth plates in fast-growing horses, epiphysitis is a complicated condition with many theories on its cause and cure. The troublesome abnormality can be exacerbated by a high-energy diet, such as the highly enriched feed normally given a horse being readied for auction.

My Lear Fan colt couldn't tolerate even one flake of alfalfa hay. No grain or other high-protein food was on the menu either. Having dealt with this particular issue many times, Darlene explained that the only option open to us was a green pasture and the grass-only, all-natural diet it provided.

At this point, I was driving six hours from Pleasanton to Visalia and back each month, ostensibly to check on his progress. But in actuality I felt a particular connection with this colt, and I really just wanted to see him. Although the foal pneumonia had cleared up in short order, the lack of improvement in the epiphysitis condition disappointed me with each trip.

But oh my goodness, was he ever a character. He was so proud of himself. The brawny, shiny colts parading around on the other side of the fence did not intimidate my ugly duckling. This son of Lear Fan was filled to bursting with a *joie de vivre,* which came to him as naturally as each blink of his eye.

First to greet visitors and the last to leave, jumping, kicking and rearing, he loved to show off. The little muskrat lookalike was truly masterful at inciting full-scale stampedes on both sides of the fence. I always traveled home smiling.

Months passed before Casual Lies could tolerate a more normal diet of grass, grain, hay and supplements without his joints swelling, but eventually he was able to join the other yearlings. No doubt about it, his fitness level elevated precipitously once he joined them in their horseplay. My train was finally back on track. The biggest question was whether or not it would reach the station in time.

~

WITH EIGHT MONTHS UNDER his belt at Darlene's Two Ton Tony resort, the epiphysitis problem had been completely resolved, and Casual Lies took his first step off the trailer and into my barn at Pleasanton in September 1990. He was bigger, stronger and a good deal gawkier than the last time I had seen him. Covered with brittle brown hair, he still brought to mind that genetically altered muskrat. At first glance, second glance and frankly any glance, he certainly didn't resemble a horse that would one day hear the roar of 137,000 fans as he took his first steps onto a historic racetrack in Louisville, Kentucky, and kept his date with destiny.

Since the major San Francisco Bay-area racetracks, Bay Meadows and Golden Gate Fields, didn't allow the breaking of horses on their premises, Jim and I made the nearby track and stables of the Alameda County Fair Association in Pleasanton, California, the year-round headquarters for our training business. Designated an auxiliary facility for all the Northern California tracks, Pleasanton offered 24-hour security, clockers to time horses' workouts six days a week and a gate crew once a week.

With the morning training activities at Pleasanton mirroring those at the major racetracks, albeit on a much smaller scale, we had an ideal facility for accomplishing our goals with the young horses in our care. We especially liked the added caveat that we could ship our ready-to-run horses

21

the same day they were scheduled to race. This enabled us to operate a full-service training and racing stable.

As part of the California fair circuit, Pleasanton had a 13-race program that featured mixed-breed racing for two weeks in late June and early July. The breeds included Thoroughbreds, Quarter Horses, Appaloosas, Arabians and mules, each type having its own races on the card. Every year we found it hilarious when the Thoroughbreds got their first look at the mules headed to the racetrack. You would think someone had trotted out a Bengal tiger the way the Thoroughbreds wheeled and bucked.

~

AN ADVANTAGE TO WORKING with a sales yearling like Stanley—a barn name, or nickname, that Jim and I soon gave him—is that he has benefitted from lessons in patience and manners. Accustomed to the daily activities around the sales barns, which are not completely dissimilar to the morning activities around a training track, yearlings with sales experience slide smoothly into their new daily routine. Bits in their mouth and wearing a blanket have become as natural to them as a second skin. Sales yearlings are, without exception, a joy to handle. . .well, that is, until our giant chipmunk came along.

Once we began the breaking process with Stanley, we found we had our hands full. Although the youngster was very sweet and loved people, he was also explosive. He could be in trouble in a blink of an eye, and if at all possible, he would gladly include you in the festivities. His friendly, curious and seemingly placid demeanor could change in an instant, and at times you sensed he deliberately used his volatility to intimidate you, even toy with you.

Stabled in the second stall down from my office, Stanley frequently turned his razor-sharp gaze on my open door. He took to snorting, stomping, pawing and bucking in place—all favorite ploys to attract attention. He especially adored scraping his teeth up and down the metal doorframe, probably because I cringed in reaction to the sound, which was worse than nails on a chalkboard. I found hollering at him to knock it off was more of an encouragement than deterrent. If I gave in and walked over to put an end to whatever he was up to, then he had certainly accomplished his mission of getting my full attention.

Unless Stanley was eating, you could rest assured he was plotting mischief. Hanging up the phone one morning, I was greeted by a rumble starting up in the second stall. I dashed over to find my fuzzy-haired heathen stampeding around the confines of the stall, dragging what remained of his blanket in his teeth.

~

IN CALIFORNIA, MOST TRAINERS expect their horses to be broke to the hot-walker machine. The majority of tracks have limited space around the barns and the shedrows themselves are too full of people doing morning chores to be a safe place to walk horses consistently. Thus the hot-walker becomes a very important and essential piece of equipment. When horses are handled correctly both in the breaking process and in the daily use of a hot-walker, the inherent dangers can be managed. It's when they're not introduced to the hot-walker correctly or monitored at all times that things can go horribly wrong.

Your typical hot-walker consists of a center-based drive mechanism, with a main shaft coming straight up from its core. Connected to the main shaft are four heavy-gauge metal arms stretching out horizontally about 10 feet. Attached to the far end of each arm is a safety quick release and a two- to three-foot shank, with a sturdy snap for attaching to each horse's halter. Viewed from above, the hot-walker would look like a plus sign.

Horses love to play on this machine. They will often rear up or buck and kick at anyone who strays too close. With four horses on a hot-walker at any one time, you really have very little control if something goes wrong. If one horse pulls back, he could start a chain reaction with the other three. Shanks break, walkers turn over, and I have even seen walker arms—sturdy industrial-strength arms—bent.

Horses can end their careers and even their lives when they become out of control on hot-walkers. Hence, proper training and manners are imperative when it comes to the hot-walker. Even so, the horses need to be supervised at all times.

One summer during evening chores at the Vallejo fair meet, a commotion started up on the walker next to mine. I hustled over, intent on lending a hand, when an Appaloosa lunged forward, then reared up, banging his head so hard that he fell to the ground. He lay there unconscious, his head and neck suspended by the hot-walker shank. The two other horses on the walker with him were completely out of control, pulling back in terror. I yelled at the grooms to get the other horses off the hot-walker. Once this had been accomplished, I pulled the quick release on the shank that held the injured horse's head off the ground.

As luck would have it, right at the end of the barn a veterinarian had just pulled up in his rig. When the horse didn't get up, the vet ran over and worked frantically to save him. I was on the ground holding the young horse's head in my lap, stroking him and trying to shield his unseeing eye from the sun. I sobbed uncontrollably as I watched the life force drain from his eye, turning gray and frosty. From that moment on, I never felt a horse was completely safe on a hot-walker, no matter how well he was trained.

Each baby was introduced to our hot-walker alone and only after the busiest part of the morning chores was done. Jim would walk with him, holding the walker shank in one hand and the lead shank in the other. Next, we would hang Brownie, our stable's lead pony, on the hot-walker with the colt we were breaking. This would help a baby get accustomed to having another horse on the machine.

Brownie was a great anchor. Muzzle wrinkled in distaste, he would practically sigh when the colts acted out. If you didn't keep yelling "get up" at Brownie, he would just stand there taking a sunbath. Stopping the hot-walker is a favorite trick, and one every horse easily learns. Indeed, Brownie made an art form of snoozing on the hot-walker.

Most horses will try pulling back on the hot-walker at least once; not so with Stanley. He seemed to take to the hot-walker quite readily during the breaking process, never posing a problem. He enjoyed walking about as if on parade, alert and enjoying the activity.

One day, for no apparent reason...bam! He was off and running, and not at just a gallop either. He was off to the races, blasting around there like a motorcycle in a pit.

Heart in my throat, I screamed "whoa" at the top of my lungs, waving my arms around like a madwoman. Jim risked his life by jumping into the middle of the melee and grabbing the hot-walker arm across from Stanley. Literally lifted off his feet and swinging free on a wild ride of his own, Jim was finally able to dig his heels in and slow the mighty Stanley down. Only at this point could I get involved and put a stop to the mayhem.

Weak-kneed, out of breath, my heart thumping painfully, I managed to clip a shank on Stanley and get him safely back to his stall. Stanley never walked, or ran for that matter, on a hot-walker again.

~

CUTS, BRUISES, EVEN BROKEN bones are a way of life for people who choose to work with horses, especially horsemen who take on the task of breaking young bloodstock to bit and saddle. With Jim's background and his amazing talent, we specialized in bringing young horses from pasture to saddling paddock or, in the case of Stanley, from a Kentucky mixed bloodstock auction to a California two-year-old-in-training sale the following year.

Since sales yearlings don't come broke to the saddle. You face at least 45 days teaching them all the basics. It takes time and patience to help young horses graduate from round corral to a covered arena, from riding the open fields and then on to the racetrack. Jim and I built our reputation on sending out well-broke, well-mannered horses.

In our barn we started all the yearlings in the same basic manner. No steps were skipped because they had been handled extensively at the sales. Saddling and bridling took place in the round corral, followed by driving with long reins threaded through the stirrups. We taught horses how to respond to pressure on the bit in their mouths, thereby giving the rider some control before he stepped on for the first time.

From the moment we saddled Stanley and watched him move, we knew I had found something special. Stanley was just so different. How do you describe something you can see but can't hear, like the beat of butterfly wings. It wasn't the how or what that made Stanley different. It was more like a bright, unseen aura. Stanley seemed to sparkle. He radiated, and he definitely had sizzle.

Often capricious, Stanley had a mercurial nature that could emerge when least expected. This became particularly evident one fine day in the round corral when Jim and I had finished a session of saddling and bridling the colt. Jim was ready to unleash the beast and drive Stanley with the long reins.

All horsemen soon learn the wisdom of not crossing behind any horse, no matter how much you trust them. Misplaced trust can kill in the horse business. Therefore, as I headed for the exit I gave Stanley a wide berth, passing cautiously in front of him while keeping a sharp eye on his body language.

Watching me as closely as I watched him, Stanley stood there all puffed up, every muscle tensed. Because I didn't trust him, I shifted my gaze to his eyes, looking for the slightest indication that liftoff was imminent. I knew the exact second Stanley decided he was going to mow me down. I saw it in his eyes, that devilish little glint signaling I was toast.

I ducked my head and tried to sprint for the gate, when—bam—I was airborne as he slammed chest-first into me. I don't know how far he drove me across the corral, but as I landed in the dirt, I braced for him to stampede over the top of me.

Stanley was able to pull this trick despite wearing above-the-knee hobbles, which hadn't slowed him down a bit.

"Are you okay?" Jim yelled as he frantically worked the reins, endeavoring to keep Stanley from trampling me.

I didn't try to move, not a twitch. Over the years, I'd learned it was prudent to move one limb at a time slowly until I found the one that hurt. Besides, being planted face down in the dirt didn't lend itself to bouncing up as if nothing had happened. And finally, I was having a little trouble sucking air back into my lungs.

It was fortunate that Stanley chose to stop and stand quietly, seemingly pleased to have included me in his idea of fun. Although I was sore all over, I was more concerned about him than myself. He'd hit me so hard that he'd popped a thumb-size split in his shoulder muscle, a dimple in the muscle he would carry for the rest of his life.

~

AT LAST THE DAY CAME when Jim declared that Stanley was ready to go to the track for the first time. I rode along on Brownie, the equine equivalent of a Heinz 57. Brownie was so long of tooth it was hard to determine his exact age—but it was well north of 22, I am sure.

Raw-boned, crotchety and afraid of plastic bags, Brownie had been rescued out of a pasture where every horse was skin and bone except himself. He must have been king of the feed trough. Brownie had also seen more than his share of obstreperous yearlings during his tenure with us. With a somewhat sour outlook on life, he simply endured his job for the most part.

Stanley, on the other hand, loved Brownie. Nipping while bumping his shoulder into Brownie, Stanley was as hard to dissuade as an ardent Pepé Le Pew.

First ventures to the track with any of the young horses were conducted just before the track officially closed, usually around 11 a.m. Generally by that time of day, only the occasional late galloper was around to startle the colts.

Over the years, you came to expect certain reactions the first time the youngsters get to the wide-open atmosphere of the racetrack. They can freeze up. Some will bust in two and buck like crazy, trying to dislodge the rider. Others will snort and prop, ducking at their own shadow. The majority of mine, however, would stick like glue to Brownie, following him wide-eyed.

The entrance to the track at Pleasanton is located near the head of the lane on the homestretch. When we took our first steps onto the racetrack, Stanley was busy aggravating both Brownie and me with his usual enthusiasm. Unfortunately, this happened to coincide exactly with a horse thundering around the turn into the homestretch.

Because I was concentrating on deflecting Stanley's never-ending game of nip and bump, I didn't have a tight hold on him. With no warning, Stanley wheeled, tore free of my grasp, and took off for the horse. Within three or four jumps from a standstill, he was head and head with this horse at a full gallop. Jim sawed on the bit to no avail. I watched in horror while Jim struggled for more than a quarter mile to pull Stanley out of his stampede.

I was also horrified as a horsewoman, because as a trainer I spent weeks conditioning a horse's muscles, tendons, ligaments, even bones before I ever asked a horse to pick up the pace down the lane. Stanley on his first trip to the racetrack had just gone heads up with an old, experienced racehorse, just short of breezing, in four jumps. No telling what kind of damage he could have done to himself. Fortunately he came out of the incident with no obvious signs of injury.

On the other hand, I was totally in awe of the colt. I had never seen a yearling that was capable of doing what Stanley had just done. He shouldn't have been able to do it either. Babies don't know how to lengthen their stride like an old campaigner. What in the world had I gotten my hands on?

The strongest youngster Jim and I had ever trained, the weedy little colt challenged us in an unending contest of wills. Determined to outrun everything that came near him, Stanley focused his pent-up energy into a single-minded purpose—full speed, straight ahead. He loved running, which was fine, but unless we could harness his explosive behavior, eventually he would injure himself, and his future wouldn't be a good one.

~

CONDITIONING YOUNG RACEHORSES is a long and involved process, without shortcuts. A slow process of change is under way every minute of every day—the bones of their legs and joints remodel as they grow over the weeks and months. These changes accelerate when the young horses go into training, and the concussion resonating up their legs intensifies with the added weight of a rider on their backs. Muscles get fit far faster than the underlying skeletal structure, and it is a common mistake to let a young horse go too fast too soon without the proper foundation.

As the days passed, Stanley became ever more determined to do what came most natural to him—run. Jim said that Stanley was fighting him every jump of the way. We discussed the problem and tried blinkers, rings and more substantial bits, all in an attempt to slow Stanley down, to regain at the very least some semblance of control. Galloping with other youngsters didn't deter Stanley. From the first step he would feel challenged and then run off, leaving them in his dust.

Eventually, we tried a ring bit, which is an awfully strong bit for a tender-mouthed yearling to tolerate. He slowed only marginally and responded by running out on the turns. He was fighting us and losing his joy, leaving only the fight.

His determination to fight got him in serious trouble one morning at the quarter pole when a horse came thundering by on the inside and Stanley responded so explosively that he blew the turn and bolted into the outside fence. He didn't go over the rail, but much to my horror, he rode it for a ways.

I raced down the outside rail, where Jim was examining a pretty nasty scrape on the colt's right knee. Jim was upset, his adrenaline pumping, and while I don't recall his exact words, several of them were of the familiar four-letter variety.

We had now zoomed past worried and had arrived at frantic. We had a colt with as much natural ability as we had ever seen, and yet we were faced with a highly unstable package of TNT.

Obviously, the more severe the bit, the harder Stanley was going to fight it. He might not have bolted into the outside fence wearing a relatively kind D-bit, but then, you couldn't slow him down with the D-bit. With a ring bit, you could slow him down, but that was the bit he was fighting when he'd made a right turn into the fence. We had tried blinkers, galloping with slower yearlings and snubbing him up to a pony, all without success. Jim was as frustrated as Stanley.

~

HORSES CAN ACQUIRE A multitude of bad habits. In the pressure-cooker atmosphere of the big racing facilities with a high volume of traffic, bad habits escalate. Bolting, rearing up, flipping, running through or over the rail and bucking are just a few examples of unacceptable behavior. Sucking back or wheeling, planting the rider head first into the dirt and then running off loose are particularly dangerous. Horses with attitude problems are a liability to themselves,

31

their riders and those around them.

A horse that dumps his rider is everyone's worst nightmare. Once horses are riderless and loose, they will run off, wildly out of control, and invariably they aim straight for another horse.

Take a moment to imagine you are galloping a horse that is up in the bit. With each stride he pulls against the restraint you are exerting on his mouth. As you round a turn on the racetrack, a riderless horse comes right at you with its reins flapping, a panicking horse running full out and whinnying in terror. You can't avoid him—he is aiming for you. Your only chance is to pull up your own horse, turn around and head in the same direction as the loose horse, mitigating the impact if he should actually hit you.

Most of these confrontations result in a near miss, but when they don't, the grim consequences of a head-on collision between two animals weighing over a thousand pounds each and at high speed doesn't bear repeating here. Jim was involved in one at the training track at Bay Meadows in the 1960s, and both horses were mortally wounded. Unless we could gain some control over Stanley, the specter of a dreadful confrontation with any horse on the racetrack, loose or not, was a reality we had to face.

~

EARLY IN OUR MARRIAGE, JIM came home from work with ugly, three-inch bloody abrasions over much of his body. He was having trouble breathing as he shoved his helmet into my hands, indicating a huge dent in the back of it. If the force of the impact is powerful enough to put a dent in a jockey helmet, Jim was incredibly lucky to be breathing, let alone standing there in front of me telling his tale. The incident brought home to me the fact that Jim could be injured even more severely than he had been, or even be killed, any morning he went to work.

The incident happened while he was galloping horses at a training farm in Norco between race meets—this I knew. They took in the horses ruled off for bad behavior at the Southern California tracks—this I hadn't known. That morning he was legged up on a filly who had arrived the previous day from Santa Anita, ruled off, but without explanation as to why.

Alert for literally anything, Jim walked her quietly to the track and backtracked at a jog, with nothing untoward happening. As any good rider knows, you don't want to tighten up or screw down, as they say, on your mount. Jim turned her, pausing, enjoying the crisp morning and relaxing before starting her gallop. The infield was lush, and cattle grazed quietly. Jim wanted her to get a good look at them. Not many Thoroughbreds have seen cattle before.

Jim was particularly good at staying on a horse that liked to wheel or suck back. What this filly did was unique and so well practiced that Jim never had a chance. Without preamble, she lunged up and forward. Experience would suggest she was going to grab the bit and run off. Instead, she dropped her head to the left, nearly to the ground. Her body followed her head around to the left, reversing direction.

What was so unusual about this move was the body drop. It left the rider suspended in the air at the end of the stirrups, momentum carrying him forward as she was turning out from under him, and headed in the opposite direction. This move was very effective at hanging the rider up in the stirrup, which is exactly what happened to Jim.

Most horses at this point would run off, dragging the rider. That would have been bad enough and perhaps deadly, but this filly turned and attacked. She kept circling, cow-kicking Jim with a hind leg and stomping him with a front hoof while he was helplessly hung up in the tack. Simultaneously, she kept trying to get down on her knees to savage him with her teeth.

"This is it," Jim thought. "I'm not getting out of this one."

After what seemed an eternity to Jim, the stirrup leather came loose. With a couple more slaps for good measure, the filly then ran off with her tail over her back, bucking and kicking. Overall, she seemed quite proud of herself.

Do you think this filly was just bad to the bone and started out with a bad attitude? I don't think so. Bad behavior becomes a bad habit the second time it happens.

Stanley was racking up bad habits rapidly, and it was critical I find a way to channel his current course in a more positive direction before he hurt himself or someone else.

"I want to try a run-out bit on him," Jim said. We didn't have one of those bits in our barn, a severe and nasty piece of equipment. The bit has a studded piece on its outside edge, which causes pain if the horse continues to push into it. In my opinion, this type of bit would only have made the situation worse.

"Okay, enough," I said. "It's obvious he's running into the pain. The more severe the bit, the harder he runs out. We need to put him back into a simple D-ring."

"First horse comes by, and he'll be off to the races," Jim replied.

I thought a moment and said, "Let's start over with a different focus." We didn't need to teach this horse to run. We needed to teach him control and patience. Stanley had to learn how to relax, even more than I did.

We went back to riding Stanley around the fields and the barn area. Jim treated him like a saddle horse, to the point of riding him in a western saddle. Aboard Brownie, I rode with them for hours around the fields. Slowly we all began to regain our composure as Stanley's sore mouth softened up, and he started to relax. Brownie? He couldn't regain what he'd never lost.

Our next step with Stanley involved hanging out around the clocker's stand, which was located on the frontside of the track near the outside rail. In the beginning, Stanley became nervous when horses worked past the stand. But with repetition, eventually he settled in alongside Brownie while Jim and I chatted with the clocker and whoever else was about. He was learning patience.

Stanley was now a pretty good saddle horse, and it was time to find out if we had a racehorse who could be controlled. Before we went back to the racetrack, I contracted with Pat Seeley, a longtime friend and good hand, to help us out. Pat would ride his saddle horse while I rode Brownie, sandwiching Stanley and Jim between us every time we went to the track. With two pony horses to love, Stanley was definitely going to be distracted.

Once on the track, Pat kept Stanley from running out while I buffered him on the inside from the horses galloping by. As time went on and Stanley stopped tensing up, I would ease Brownie off and charge up, challenging Stanley repeatedly while Pat kept the colt from bolting out. The final step was to get another rider to gallop a racehorse up to Stanley, going head and head for a couple of furlongs, then pull away.

It took time, patience and consistency, but after a couple of months, I finally stopped holding my breath when a horse galloped or breezed past our trio. Stanley had become responsive to his rider, rather than his instincts, and he became one of the best-behaved horses on the track.

Cheerful, curious and mischievous, Stanley was back. Still annoying when he put his mind to it, he also lit up my life and the shedrow with his enormous energy. I couldn't wait to get to the barn in the morning to see Stanley's brilliant eyes locked on mine, willing me to fill his bucket first. And I always did.

~

WHEN THE BARRETTS TWO-year-old-in-training sale finally came around in March, my ugly duckling was still homely. But what a runner he was. It still makes my scalp tingle to think about those early days, when we would breeze him gently down the lane with other colts. Stanley barely had to get out of a gallop to go head and head with another horse.

Barretts stabled us adjacent to D. Wayne Lukas and his tastefully presented consignment of well-bred horses. As a result, few people ever got as far as our barn. It remains surprising to me that so few people at the Barretts sale couldn't see enough value in Stanley's catalog page to even take a look at my horse.

Already fully aware of the gender bias in the Thoroughbred industry, I listed my name on the catalog page as S. L. Riley Training Stables. One guy who stopped by the barn asked, "S. L. Riley? Who is he?"

I responded, "He is me. Would you like to see the colt out of the stall?"

His response was a simple "No," and he wandered back to Wayne's consignment.

When it was Stanley's turn to go to the walk ring prior to entering the sale pavilion, I recall a contingent of gentlemen dressed all in black, very cool looking and attracting a lot of attention. Accompanied by Wayne Lukas, they were scanning the sales catalog and watching the horses parade prior to entering the auction ring. I learned it was rapper M.C. Hammer and his entourage.

Lukas told me later that he had met Hammer at Santa Anita one afternoon in the VIP box-seat area of the Turf Club. Hammer was obviously enjoying the afternoon wagering on the races, and Wayne struck up a conversation with him. He suggested as the afternoon went on that if Hammer liked betting on the horses, he should take a chance on buying a horse to race. As a result of that conversation by the time the sale was concluded, Hammer had bought at least one horse from Lukas.

When the hammer came down on Stanley, however, he was still mine—final bid, $45,000. This was simply not a price I could accept for my special colt. Disgruntled we headed home a little wiser about two-year-old-in-training sales. If I wanted my horses to be seen I would have to consign them with a trainer who had better credentials than I, preferably a man, since that seemed to be what the buyers expected to see on the catalog page.

After the sale, which turned out to be yet another expensive lesson, I decided to turn Casual Lies out and let him grow, with the intention of bringing him back to train for a late summer and fall campaign.

Confident in my talented horse, I didn't hesitate to write the check to nominate him to the Hollywood Futurity, a prestigious graded race for first-class two-year-olds run in December at Hollywood Park in Southern California. There would be plenty of time to get some racing in him before we ventured down to where the best of the best hung out.

Chapter Three

A Horse with Two Names

So why the name Stanley? People have asked me that nearly as often as I've been questioned about the story behind his registered name, Casual Lies. His official registration papers from The Jockey Club designated him as "Un-named Lear Fan colt," and in the beginning we just called him the Lear Fan colt.

I always designated a barn name for every horse I trained. I strongly believe that a name personalizes each horse as an individual and reminds everybody involved that the horses are not just business commodities. Two or 20, each horse has a different personality, and they each have different likes and dislikes. Stanley, for instance, would have been ecstatic if you had parked yourself outside his stall, entertaining him 24/7.

The total opposite of Stanley was a Quarter Horse sent to me from Southern California's Los Alamitos racetrack to run at the Santa Rosa track on the fair-racing circuit of Northern California. I don't recall his registered name, but I can still visualize him perfectly because of his barn name. He ran in 870-yard races, just a few yards short of a half mile and the Quarter Horse equivalent of a route race.

This guy simply wanted to be left alone and was more than willing to fight about it. He was massive, hammer-headed and raw boned, taking up a huge amount of the stall. When he wasn't eating or drinking, he stood perfectly still, catty-corner, eyes closed and one hind leg cocked. Every muscle twitch was an implied threat. His muzzle was always crinkled up in distaste, the equine equivalent of a sneer. By the end of the first day, I had nicknamed him Crank.

Crank was no youngster, and he was completely set in his ways. He refused to change anything without a battle. You could go in and clean Crank's stall, but you better be quick about it. In fact, he seemed to have a time limit for how long each foray into his stall should take. If he needed to be brushed or saddled, you took the equipment in and did the job while he stood there, ears pinned and tail switching. If you dared to pet him, he was on you in a heartbeat, teeth bared and massive body prepared for an assault.

Crank never—and I mean never—put his head out the stall door. He definitely had my number, he correctly read my anxiety, and he intimidated me whenever I had to go anywhere near him. Jim handled him for the most part, and they seemed to understand each other. Jim wasn't much into petting, and he wasn't about to take any guff from Crank.

There was a reward for putting up with the horse's cantankerous nature, however. Crank never finished worse than second for us in every race he ran that summer.

Crank and Stanley illustrate why you must treat each horse as an individual. Even though training has its basics, you have to be willing to adjust for each situation. You can't train them all the same, nor expect the same result from any particular method.

I always looked for a recognizable personality quirk that would guide me when it came to nicknames. The right nickname would make a horse recognizable for everyone who worked in my barn. If I told the vet we were going to give Crank a vitamin shot, he knew conversation would not be taking place in the stall.

Once my Lear Fan colt arrived at my barn to start his training, he needed a nickname. As to the why of Stanley, I can only say he could have been a Buddy or a Chubs or even a Fritz. On occasion when he was particularly annoying, another name or two comes to mind as well. However, Stanley seemed to suit him, and it stuck.

An official name—one that would be notable and appropriate—was going to take more time and thought. Recognizing early on how really special Stanley was, I wanted his registered name to be memorable. Once we picked a name we would then face the daunting paper gauntlet of applications, rejections and more applications before we would get the ultimate approval from The Jockey Club.

Many thousands of horses are born each year, and inevitably the day will come when an official name must be registered with The Jockey Club. It's not as easy as you might imagine naming a horse. The American version of The Jockey Club was established in 1894, and they have developed very strict guidelines when it came to names.

No more than 18 letters, punctuation and spaces counting as a letter. No initials and the name can't end in a numerical designation. You can't use a person's name, famous or not, without their permission. Names of "notorious" persons or trademarks, stable names, vulgar or obscene words, famous or well-known horses are banned as well.

I particularly enjoyed the oft-repeated story of one man who ran smack into the name-game challenge. Truth or fiction, the tale gives a good idea how difficult the process can be.

As the story goes, the gentleman submitted three names with first, second and third preferences indicated on the first application he mailed to The Jockey Club. Submitting more than one name, he felt confident he would get a name that he wanted. In remarkably short order, by return mail, he received his original application with all three choices marked *unavailable*.

Bitterly disappointed when he was unable to get one of his first three choices, he dutifully chose and submitted three more names, only to see the application returned to him once again, marked with the familiar *unavailable* next to each of his second-choice names.

Now thoroughly discouraged, frustrated and perhaps a little testy, on his next application he submitted only one name for consideration: "Unavailable." One can only imagine what he had to say when the official communication from The Jockey Club arrived and "Unavailable" was marked *unavailable*.

~

FOR MANY PEOPLE, THE NAME their horse carries is nearly as important as owning the horse itself. Incorporating part of the sire or dam's name is one approach, or perhaps using parts of both. Some people push the limits of propriety. For instance, a horse ran many years ago named Piaonya, pronounced with three syllables, PEE-on-ya. Though his sire was Pia Star, it's clear where they were going with that name.

Some owners like to reference something they sacrificed to obtain their horse, like Brent's Trans Am or Mom's Ferrari. Many a horse has been named after a favorite pet. With permission, a famous person's name can be used. Chris Evert was a champion on the tennis courts, and her equine namesake was equally great on the racetrack. Names are picked up from movies, like Bodacious Tatas, a graded stakes winner of over $430,000, her name a reference to a line in the film *An Officer and a Gentleman*.

Inspiration for naming a horse can come from just about anywhere. In the days leading up to the Kentucky Derby, and after the crowd of reporters around my barn in Louisville had thinned out considerably one morning, my gaze landed on a slightly stooped gentleman in a brown suit. He carried a very battered old-fashioned briefcase in one hand, and he was carefully making his way to my barn. Without giving it a second thought, I pulled back the barrier barring entry to my end of the shedrow and waved him in. The man stepped into the shedrow without hesitation. It was quite obvious that the man had found his quarry—me.

Pausing, he peered at me through heavy dark eyebrows. His quizzical expression lasted long enough to give me the distinct feeling I was being gauged. As I soon came to learn, I was in the presence of turf writing royalty, Joe Hirsch of the *Daily Racing Form*. Joe, who had often been referred to as the dean of Thoroughbred racing writers, was a truly remarkable character. Even so many years after his death, I still cherish that quiet meeting we enjoyed together.

Feeling instantly at ease, I invited Joe into my temporary tack room and office combo, where we pulled up a couple of plastic lawn chairs for an impromptu interview. The only thing is, I'm not sure who was interviewing whom.

Deep voice rumbling gently, Joe shared his stories in a paced cadence. He was literally a walking, talking horse racing encyclopedia. A well-practiced and talented ambassador for racing, Joe made me feel as though we had been friends for years, as he had done with so many interviewees before me.

The naming of Casual Lies came up, and Joe shared the following story with me. Hall of Fame trainer Hirsch Jacobs was staying at the old Brown Hotel in Louisville during Derby week. At that time, the 1950s, Louisville had only three hotels, Joe remarked. The walls between the rooms of the Brown Hotel were so paper thin that they offered very little privacy. On every day of Jacobs's stay he was entertained, whether he wanted to be or not, by someone repeatedly playing the song "Personality" and singing along with alacrity. Day in, day out, over and over again, the song's lyrics pounded through the walls into Jacobs's room and into his head: "'Cause you got personality, walk—personality, talk—personality, smile—personality. . ."

Jacobs vowed if he ever got a horse good enough to run in the Kentucky Derby, he would name it Personality. Not only was Personality good enough to compete, he finished third in the 1970 Kentucky Derby, won the Preakness Stakes and ultimately was named champion three-year-old of that year. Unfortunately, Hirsch Jacobs died before he could see his talented horse run in the Derby.

Joe shared many great stories with me that day in Kentucky, just the two of us in plastic chairs camped out in a borrowed tack room, reliving memorable moments from Joe's past. He had conversed with so many historically notable people throughout his amazing career, had even shared an apartment with American professional football Hall of Famer Joe Namath for 11 years, and yet there we sat, quaintly chatting like old friends.

Here I was, the lady from the suburbs who had committed what many would have considered a folly, refinancing her house to buy a racehorse prospect and having the temerity to bring the horse to Kentucky for the Derby. Yet Joe did not find the story at all incongruous. He gave me advice on several levels, not the least of which was how to handle the press.

"Always hold something safe, Shelley. Don't give it all to them." Then he added with that toothy smile he could flash in an instant, "Present company excluded, of course."

~

SOME HORSES ARE NAMED TO make a social statement. I have often wondered who named Judge Smells, which led to an unfortunate choice for one of his offspring, Smelly. One of my personal favorites was Cat Ballou and her daughters, Pussy Paws and Kitty Klaus.

I have discovered through personal experience that it is unwise to name a horse after a dead relative. The horse must prove worthy of carrying the memory of your departed loved one. Invariably, when he fails do so, another layer is added to your disappointment.

I once trained for a gentleman who, when told his colt really needed to be gelded, responded with an explosive NO! He went on to explain that he'd named the colt after his brother Joe, who had died the same year this colt was born. Furthermore, he and his brother both believed in reincarnation. Therefore, he simply couldn't geld the colt just in case it was his brother. Joe would simply never forgive him.

For whatever reason a horse is named, ultimately a good horse makes for a great name. Farma Way is not particularly a great-sounding name. But factor in a brilliant dose of speed, a tremendous desire to win and nearly $3 million in earnings, and the name sounds terrific.

~

ANOTHER UNQUESTIONABLY GREAT trainer, D. Wayne Lukas, over the years had the opportunity to be involved with a large number of horses who ultimately ran themselves into a position of greatness and a great name. Wah La, Lady's

Secret, Dream Team, Twilight Agenda, Winning Colors and Landaluce were just a few of the exceptional horses he trained.

One morning I asked Wayne about his favorite names and how he came up with them. He said that his number one criterion was a fun story behind the name, not whether the name itself is catchy.

Wayne recalled how one name developed as the result of a horse sale. He explained that when he attends a sale, he doesn't like to look at the catalog page before he examines the horses. He feels that the breeding on the page may color his opinion of the individual standing in front of him.

While attending a sale at Saratoga in New York, he and his son, Jeff, were inspecting a filly that Wayne instantly liked overall because she was balanced, correct and athletic.

"Everything fits," he said to Jeff. "Go ahead, take a look and see who she's by."

When Jeff turned to the appropriate catalog page, he said, "She's by a first-year sire, Deputy Minister."

"Well, let's try and keep an open mind," Wayne replied. "She's got everything we want physically."

After having bought the filly, Wayne ran into the name-game tango, like so many others have. Being turned down on no less than eight names by The Jockey Club, he thought back to that afternoon in Saratoga and recalled his remark to Jeff. Thus, Open Mind was named and went on to be a two-time champion, confirming Wayne's eye for conformation, great instincts and penchant for coming up with a good name.

~

HALL OF FAME TRAINER Charlie Whittingham, an enthusiastic purveyor of countless numbers of great racing stories, told me one of his favorites about naming a horse. He and Mary Jones Bradley were partners on a colt who was nearly ready to run in his first race and therefore desperately needed an official name. Mrs. Bradley, who was living in New York and was certainly no stranger to the challenges involved in naming a horse, had submitted several names to The Jockey Club, all of which had been subsequently turned down. Finally in frustration, and I can only imagine with not just a tiny bit of humor, she submitted the name "Whittingham" for the colt. The name was accepted and made official by The Jockey Club.

When Mrs. Bradley told Charlie that she had named the horse Whittingham, Charlie said—I'm sure with that wonderfully ever-present twinkle in his eye—"Well, we'll see. If he can't run, I'm sure he must have been named after my brother Joe."

As time went by and Charlie prepared the horse to run at Santa Anita, it became apparent that he indeed had quite a bit of talent.

According to Charlie, Joe Hernandez, the racecaller known as the Voice of Santa Anita Park from the time the track opened in 1934, liked to take the occasional flutter and wager on the horses. So Charlie wasn't exactly surprised when Hernandez appeared at his side on the day Whittingham was scheduled to run in his first race and asked if Charlie thought his namesake had a chance in that afternoon's race. Charlie responded that he felt the colt would run well that day.

As Hernandez called the race later that afternoon, he worked his way through the field as announcers do: *"And it's Whittingham, well off the pace."* As the race proceeded, *"Whittingham is fifth and moving up."* As the field came down the lane and Whittingham started moving strongly on the leaders, Hernandez yelled, *"And here comes Charlie, and Charlie's going to win!"* Thus, Whittingham was a Charlie and not a brother Joe.

~

WHAT IS IT ABOUT NAMING horses that inspires so many stories and subsequently so many questions? Of course the truth is always the best way to proceed, but in fact the whole truth is not completely necessary in all cases, nor kind for that matter.

The most popular story on the reason I named my colt Casual Lies, and the one I encouraged the most, concerned a young woman who worked with me on the dispatch radio at the Sacramento County Sheriff's Department shortly before I started training horses. She asked me about a dress she was wearing.

"Shelley, what do you think? I made it myself," she asked as she twirled about in front of me. I was sitting in front of the radio at the time with nearly 60 units responding to my calls. I glanced over and felt my mouth freeze up in a round "O" of surprise.

A momentary lull in the usual busy radio traffic meant that I could not put off my answer. She was obviously proud of her creation, and she posed expectantly, undoubtedly awaiting my gushing admiration.

The dress was hideous. It was made from some kind of waffle-stamped cotton and covered with huge intersecting round blotches of loud colors. The sundress styling harkened back to Rosie the Riveter on her day off at the beach, complete with headscarf to match.

My jaw was wagging, but nothing was coming out until, "Ohhh. . .wow, it's, umm, green, and that turquoise. . .my goodness, what a pretty color of pink. Oh and that yellow, uh, you should always wear yellow. It really suits you." I stumbled and gushed along, and she seemed pleased.

I told my casual lie so as not to hurt her feelings. Was this the true story behind my naming Stanley Casual Lies? It certainly could have been, and it would have been easy to leave it as the whole truth at this point. But, alas, it would have been a lie.

The next true story behind the trail of half truths regarding the inspiration behind the name Casual Lies involved a four-way conversation that took place in my shedrow. The discussion concerned one horse in particular who was racing that day and trained by a rather well known trainer, and as circumstance would have it, the horse was stabled in my barn. The exchange was filled with half-truths, evasions and a few observations that skirted dangerously along the edge of becoming outright lies. When the conversation concluded and Jim and I walked away, I shook my head and said to him, "Oh how casually we lie."

I stopped dead in my tracks. Jim continued walking down the shedrow until he realized I was no longer beside him. He turned as I said, "Geez, that would make a great name for a horse."

"No way; surely it's already been used," he said. "There's definitely no chance we'd be able to get it through The Jockey Club."

"You never know."

I sent it in, and lo and behold, two weeks later it was official: Stanley was Casual Lies. I didn't even send in a second choice. I think it was quite possibly the first time I got a name approved on the very first application I submitted.

So is the second story the true one behind the official name I came up with for Stanley? I will tell you this—the second story is very close to the complete truth, with only the particulars of the conversation left out that triggered my moment of inspiration.

I switched rather easily between Stanley, Lear Fan colt and Casual Lies. As a progression, I bought a Lear Fan colt, I remember Casual Lies, but I *knew* Stanley.

~

ANOTHER INTERESTING STORY I heard along the way was that the name for the 1994 movie *True Lies*, starring Arnold Schwarzenegger and Jamie Lee Curtis and directed by James Cameron, was originally going to be called *Casual Lies*. When the filmmakers discovered that there was a horse by that name, they felt they had to change the movie title. I don't know if that is a true story or a true lie, but it is a fun rumor to share.

By now you can see how difficult and trying it can be to come up with a registered name for a Thoroughbred. When you name a horse, and particularly when it involves something that is important to you on any level, you inevitably feel more engaged and more invested in the career and success of that horse.

When your horse's name is being called out over the roar of the crowd as he thunders down the lane, it is always exciting. Is it even more exciting when you have picked the name out yourself? It always was for me.

And yet, when the name being called on the loudspeaker over the roar of the crowd was Casual Lies, my voice could be heard screaming—"Come on, Stanley!"

Chapter Four

Learning How to Win

I like winning races, any races, even at the lowest level of racing: claiming races, where a horse can be purchased, or claimed, for the stated claiming price, which might be as low as $2,000 or as high as $100,000. Winning a claiming race with a horse after months of hard work satisfies and excites me.

Winning a stakes race—the prized top-class racing event—ranks even higher, and the thrill definitely lasts longer. Those seconds and thirds aren't shabby results either, but rarely, if ever, do they equal the thrill of the win.

When getting into the horse racing business, the most common tendency is to get too high on your horse right from the beginning. Horses come in many levels of ability, just like human athletes. Your willpower cannot transform a horse into the next Secretariat. If you want to own a winner, you must accept an animal's limitations and run him at a competitive level where he can be the best.

The new colts that came into my barn with their big, curious eyes and endearing innocence represented new opportunities to me. Embracing the concept of infinite possibilities, I didn't start each day with a cynical or jaundiced view, especially where my untried youngsters were concerned. Ultimately if their ability indicated they were destined to run with the far easier company found in a $12,500 maiden claiming race, I recognized and accepted that. But for me, part of the joy of coming to the barn each morning included the possibility that any one in the row of faces anxiously awaiting their rations of grain could be my very first stakes horse. I frequently compared yearlings to blank chalkboards, where the equation had yet to take shape and I held the chalk. I always felt blessed to have both the chance and privilege to affect their futures.

Over the years, Jim gave me considerable flack for this point of view. He was more of a pessimist, or perhaps a realist would be more accurate. He always hoped they would be talented and tough enough just to break their maidens.

Horses who have never won a race are called maidens and usually run with other horses that haven't won a race either. You only get to break your maiden once, and it is the easiest money you'll ever earn. The racing only gets tougher the more races you win.

~

IN THE LATE SPRING OF 1991, Stanley's training progressed steadily. He grew and filled out at an increasingly rapid pace. What had taken so long to begin was happening so fast now it was a wonder you weren't hearing his frame crackling and popping as it expanded. When I tacked him up in the morning, it seemed like I had to switch to a bigger girth on a weekly basis.

As we trained toward his first race, the distances we galloped and worked him lengthened and quickened. However, we didn't have any two-year-olds in our barn with enough talent to go with him, and for that reason, he wasn't getting enough out of his works. Asking a first-time starter to race in the afternoon without proper fitness and plenty of experience working with other horses wouldn't be a good idea.

Carefully I selected older, seasoned workout partners for my promising two-year-old, partners chosen specifically for their willingness to work head and head. I would not want to jeopardize Stanley's future just to out-work a cheap claimer. Blasting around the track going five-eighths of a mile in 58 seconds flat wasn't going to be any more helpful toward getting Casual Lies ready for a race than going too slow had been. Many a two-year-old has shin-bucked by working too fast, too soon, and my horses didn't shin-buck, something I attribute to the way we conditioned them.

Shin-bucking occurs when the bones of an adolescent Thoroughbred haven't finished remodeling. The front of the cannon bone will thicken when the pressure of a young horse's galloping and working under the weight of a rider causes a wavelike movement in the bone. As the bone remodels, it produces layers of fine web-like calcium threads, which will eventually fill in completely and stop the wave in the bone. When a young horse works too fast and the new fibers have not grown strong, these threads of calcium will break. The resulting inflammation is called shin-bucking, which is essentially a fractured cannon bone.

You can turn the young horse out, and the inflammation will go away, the pain will stop and the fibers will heal. However, when you stop the added pressure on the bone, the remodeling and maturing of the bone also stops. I found it was better to never let a horse shin-buck in the first place, so I conditioned my two-year-olds a little differently than most people, avoiding fast works early on. Slower works closer together equaled happy shins.

A mare in my barn named Miss Classy Ana was a good example of a seasoned old campaigner who frequently worked so fast that she was unsuitable as a workout companion for a young horse. One morning while preparing for a $6,200 claiming race, she worked five-eighths of a mile in :56 4/5 in front of the clocker. The clocker worked for the association that was running the current race meet, and it was his job to record the official workouts daily, information that was then made available to the betting public.

I almost dropped my stopwatch because Miss Classy Ana had done the work so easily. Trust me, if I had known she was going to work like that, it wouldn't have been in front of the clocker.

When I looked at the clocker, he was shaking his stopwatch. Then he met my eyes.

"Did you catch that?" he asked hesitantly.

"I don't know. Did you?"

"I think my watch is acting up. I am going to switch to my backup watch. What did you catch her in?"

"1:01 4/5," I said, looking at him tentatively, in a mildly questioning tone of voice.

"You sure?"

I tried again: "1:02 4/5? My watch finger isn't particularly reliable either, I may not have caught her at the right pole."

"Track's pretty slow today, and that may be the black-letter work for the morning," he responded.

A black-letter work was the fastest work of the day and was designated by a bullet point and boldface type in the *Daily Racing Form*, a popular racing publication. Each distance had a black-letter work for the day, but it didn't really signify much unless it was notably faster than the other workouts for the day.

"Track's that slow, huh? Oh well." I replied.

I wasn't worried about Classy being claimed off a black-letter 1:02 4/5 workout. A :56 4/5, however, would have had the trainers lined up to claim her. There were definite advantages to training at the auxiliary track, even if they weren't always particularly kosher.

Horses didn't often run as fast in the afternoon races as Classy could work in the morning, but then, neither did Classy. Although she was relaxed in the morning and worked faster than a lot of first-class stakes horses, she became anxious and nervous in the afternoon. The mare could lose the race before it even began, her anxiety getting the better of her, and consequently she was a perfect example of a horse who needed to be run way below her level of talent.

~

ALONG WITH PROPER CONDITIONING through galloping and workouts, perhaps the single most important aspect of getting horses ready to run in their first race—and take a big step toward learning how to win—is the starting gate. Races can be lost behind the gate, in the gate and as the gate opens.

Behind the gate while the horses wait to be loaded, they are milling around in close quarters with all the other horses and ponies gathered together. Once the loading starts, the real excitement begins. Thousand-pound equine athletes, primed and ready to explode, are shoved into a confining steel chute. Jockeys are yelling at the top of their lungs, and the men on the gate crew are rushing excitable Thoroughbreds into the stalls of the starting gate as fast as they can. The horses already in the gate are dancing in place, kicking and rearing up. Occasionally, one will flip and get stuck under the gate. Injury or even death can result from starting gate mishaps, a specter that jockeys and all other horsemen live with until the field is safely away.

A young colt that willingly walks into a horse trailer will in all likelihood be good about walking into the starting gate for the first time, and this was certainly the case with Stanley. Once in the starting gate, however, he turned into a bully. He would wallow all over the stall, squatting and leaning heavily against the sides of the gate trying to squash the rider's legs. He also tried biting the gateman and cold-cocking him with his head. Was anything ever going to be easy with Stanley?

Fortunately, Jim had a great working relationship with the gate crew. Every time they came to Pleasanton, we were at the gate with Stanley, sometimes for more than an hour. Each day Stanley was scheduled to gallop, we reinforced his weekly schooling from the gate crew by backtracking him to the starting gate, where Jim and I would school him ourselves. Hard work and consistency were the only answers with our bullheaded equine adolescent.

The day was fast approaching when a decision needed to be made about where Casual Lies would run in his first race. Logistically, our choices were to run him in Southern California at either Del Mar or Hollywood Park or in Northern California, where the fair circuit was in full swing. Naturally it was very tempting to take him to Southern California, where the purses were roughly two to three times bigger than Northern California purses.

Stanley's headstrong nature and immaturity had to be a part of my decision-making. The one thing that I knew for sure—we could still count on Stanley doing something inappropriate at the most inopportune moment.

Maiden special weight races in Southern California were going to be considerably tougher to win than a similar race on the fair circuit. Making up for mistakes brought about by Stanley being an unseasoned and unpredictable first-time starter would be especially difficult no matter where he made his maiden outing, of course.

I was confident and yet eager and nervous about my wonderful horse. Vacillating back and forth, weighing the pros and cons over and over again, I finally chose Santa Rosa County Fair. Jim heartily agreed that this would be the best track to start Casual Lies on his racing career. Our accumulated experience with Mr. Volatility incarnate told us this was a wise decision. We had plenty of time later to venture into the southland with a more mature horse who had at least a modicum of racing experience.

Besides, Santa Rosa County Fair is my favorite fair. The grounds are located amongst majestic redwoods, and the wonderful smell of redwood mixes with all the other aromas, sounds and activities one associates with an old-time county fair. You can find 4-H exhibits between the barns and the grandstand, separated from the racetrack proper by the test barn, receiving barn and saddling paddock. The sound of farm animals is quite distinct, and along with the mouth-watering smell of cotton candy and popcorn, your imagination can easily transport you back to a far gentler time.

I love the whisper of the wind high in the canopy of the massive redwoods, particularly after the races are over and the farm animals are settling down in their pens for the night. The heat of the day has passed, leaving the comforting moist warmth of evening. Squares of light cast from the brightly lit stalls highlight the darkened shedrow, framing the shadows cast by the racehorses seeking a few morsels of food they may have missed as they snuffle through their straw. There is nothing like sitting with a cold drink and soaking in the tranquility at the end of another busy day.

The next big decision regarded which jockey I would ask to ride Stanley. I wanted a young, aggressive rider, one who wouldn't be intimidated if Casual Lies ran greenly. Some of the more successful riders, who had been around for a few years, tended to be cautious on first-time starters and not inclined to do any schooling. A friend on the gate crew recommended Chance Rollins, a young rider from Phoenix. Chance was a tough kid who had been active on the rodeo circuit while cutting his teeth riding races in the bushes before he graduated to the area's major racetrack, Turf Paradise in Phoenix.

Bush meets can range from literally two lines drawn in the sand to a very small race meet on a secondary circuit. I have been at bush meets in Oklahoma with a four-stall starting gate, no grandstand and a racecaller on a bullhorn. It was easy to relate to Chance Rollins since he mirrored my husband's background and the way Jim gained enough experience to be accepted on the California Quarter Horse circuit.

The word on the backside was that Chance had been a smart and talented rider in Phoenix. He was young, bold and cocky—just like my horse. I contacted his agent, and they agreed to ride Casual Lies.

The day finally arrived, and after Jim and I completed the morning's chores in Pleasanton, we loaded up Casual Lies and Miss Classy Ana in the trailer for the two-to three-hour trip to Santa Rosa. Along with Stanley, I had entered Classy to run at Santa Rosa because she had always liked the racing surface there.

I had raised Classy myself, and after that :56 4/5 work, we were expecting her to run a very big race. I stashed a wad of cash in my pocket to bet on both my horses to win.

Gauging how well Classy would run started with the trailer ride. Classy could leave her best race in the trailer, saddling paddock, post parade or the warm-up before the race. She could wash out at any one of these junctures or all of them, and if she did, she had pretty much washed away her best chance to win as well.

Washing out is a condition arising in horses so severely anxious that they sweat until it literally runs off in a steady stream from head to tail. Lathering up, a byproduct of this sweating, occurs when patches or streams of white foam appear on anxiety-ridden horses. If the jockey had to use the whip as a sweat scraper on Miss Classy Ana, peeling sheets of white foam off her as she went behind the starting gate, you'd best keep your money in your pocket. If she appeared cool and walked quietly beside the pony, run—don't walk—to the betting window and hope the line isn't too long.

Miss Classy Ana was a beautiful and powerful filly, fast as lightning, but timid and very feminine. She would usually open up several lengths running as hard as she could until she had nothing left. You simply could not rate her. Because she would run out of gas, staggering down the lane, she collected a lot of seconds and thirds. Your only chance for a win was to get Classy to relax and not hit her endlessly with a whip.

I had decided a female jockey would provide a gentler hand for Classy. Monica Stanley was one of the first "girl riders" on the fairs and had agreed to ride my nervous mare. I watched Classy like a hawk as she settled in to walk beside her pony and arrived behind the gate. She couldn't have been drier if she were sleeping in her stall. I turned and ran to that pari-mutuel window to bet my mare to win.

Classy broke well under Monica, and they had the lead down the backstretch, but not by much. Was Monica trying to rate Classy? I didn't think that was such a good idea. About halfway around the turn for home in the 5 1/2-furlong race, Monica and Classy were a short neck in front. The late-running horses were lining up to make their move.

Classy had gone off at more than 11-1, but I wasn't counting my winnings yet. In most of her races, my mare usually led the field by a couple of lengths and barely hung on down the lane. With only a neck lead as they turned for home, I wasn't feeling good about the outcome of the race.

The crowd noise was picking up, and Jim yelled in my ear, "Look at her ears—she's pricking her ears." Horses giving all they have in a race will usually pin their ears back, not prick them forward as Classy was doing.

"Look at Monica—is she talking to her?" Jim yelled to me.

"She is, and it looks like Classy's listening," I said, seeing through my binoculars that her ears were wiggling back and forth.

Coming down the lane, the ear wiggling continued, and Classy started to pull away. She won by a couple of lengths, and I knew we had the perfect pairing with Monica and Classy. Monica told me in the winner's circle that she sang to Classy, not only in the post parade, but all the way around the course, never once hitting her with the whip. When they passed the quarter pole, Monica said she had called out to her, "Now, Classy, run now." Just like in *My Friend Flicka*, Classy did as she was asked.

Monica never told me what she sang to Classy. After all it didn't really matter, the result couldn't have been better.

~

BEING A LITTLE LEERY ABOUT how Stanley would behave when it came time for his race, I asked longtime friend Ron Hawkins to saddle him while I supervised. Ron, like Jim, was the genuine article when it came to being a good ol' cowboy. He was tall and thin, wore tight Wranglers, had a bushy handlebar mustache and always had a big chunk of chewing tobacco tucked between his cheek and gum. With snappy blue eyes and a toothy grin that flashed at the end of every sentence, Ron was a very likable guy and, not unlike Jim,

59

probably 150 years out of his time. Together they would have cut a wide swath through the Wild West.

When we approached the saddling paddock, Stanley was alert and behaving rather well, considering that he could hear pigs oinking, sheep blatting and cows lowing at full pitch. Watching all the strange activity seemed to be keeping Stanley distracted rather than winding up his motor.

Jim led Stanley around the saddling paddock with the majority of the other two-year-olds entered in the race. The jockey's valet appeared with the tack, which consisted of a postage stamp-sized jockey saddle, numbered saddlecloth, overgirth and. . . .Oh no, how could I forget? The overgirth! I had forgotten to school Stanley with an overgirth in his stall in Pleasanton the day before the race. Of all the horses for me to forget to put an overgirth on, it had to be Stanley!

In a race, jockeys ride with much smaller saddles, which have a tendency to slip off the horse's withers. To overcome this problem, the girth and overgirth are made of heavyweight elastic, not unlike two giant rubber bands.

The trouble was you couldn't predict if a horse would buck when introduced to this unfamiliar piece of equipment. So acquainting them prior to their first race was essential. I had never forgotten to do this—ever. I glanced over at Ron and the valet with a look of consternation.

Jim, who shared my blame for not schooling Stanley with the overgirth, was holding the colt's lead shank, so he would be the one who would take the brunt of the consequences if there were any. Stanley wasn't a weedy little colt anymore; he was a powerfully muscled and very explosive athlete. I have never seen anyone tiptoe around saddling a horse like Jim, Ron and the valet did that afternoon, obviously prepared for anything.

With the experience of Stanley mowing me down when

we were first breaking him still fresh in my memory, I decided the better part of valor was to step around the six-foot high divider into the next stall over. Ostensibly, I was giving the boys more room to do their job, but truthfully I didn't want to get run over again, just in case things went south.

Ed Moger Jr., who trained the horse in the next stall, gave me a rather strange look as I crept around the partition while peering anxiously over my shoulder from whence I'd come. When I explained the situation, he laughed and admitted he had done the same thing himself once or twice.

It was more than a little embarrassing when the paddock judge stepped over to me, resplendent in his off-white Panama hat and asked, "You saddling this horse too?" His eyebrows raised high, sarcasm evident in his voice.

Suppressing a nervous laugh, I said "No, just chatting with my neighbor." I certainly didn't want to admit to the paddock judge that I had forgotten to familiarize my first-time starter with an overgirth.

As I watched Ron pull the girth tight, I could see Stanley roll his eyes and sidle around a bit. But what really alarmed me was the way he was swelling up. Cautiously I leaned around the edge of the partition and suggested they take him for a turn around the paddock before they put on the overgirth. I was trying to be helpful but from well within the safety of my borrowed bunker.

The first step is the worst one, and as Stanley followed Jim out of the stall, he was puffed up with a bow in his back and his tail pinned down, like a horse that was about to break in two and buck like crazy. He didn't buck, but neither did he relax when they added the overgirth.

When Chance showed up, I warned him about the overgirth issue. The rider burst out with a roar of laughter.

He was perfect for my horse. I had discussed the race with him the day before, so my only instructions, other than win, were to be sure he warmed Stanley up thoroughly to get him used to the feel of the overgirth, hoping the colt would become comfortable with it and not buck coming out of the gate.

Before Chance climbed aboard, he shared a rumor going around the jockeys' room about trainer Doug Utley having a real runner in the race. Doug had brought a colt named Northern Tract up from Southern California to break his maiden. He considered this horse to be a future stakes horse and expected him to win off by many lengths. Yikes, so much for picking an easy race.

Stanley stayed pretty puffed up until Jim handed him off to the pony girl, but thank goodness he never bucked. He was totally taken with a new pony horse to amuse him, and everything went fairly well from that point to the final loading in the gate.

Always a tense time for me, I am generally holding my breath until the last horse is loaded in the gate and they get away safely. As the gate clanged open, I expelled my breath in a whoosh and was pleased to see Stanley running down the backstretch about midpack. This lasted for about a quarter of a mile of the 5 1/2-furlong race. At that point, leave it to Stanley to begin running erratically, losing the smooth cadence of his stride, switching leads and changing lanes.

"What's he doing?" I asked Jim in a panic. "Is he breaking down?"

"No, he's just running green, I think," he replied.

As they rounded the turn, I could see Stanley still running a bit erratically. However, Chance found a path through the horses as they bunched up.

Coming into the lane, Stanley was in fifth place, and Chance took the opportunity to take him to the outside of horses. Once he got my big colt straightened out, Stanley overcame his confusion, galloped strongly by the field and won by a widening two lengths over Northern Tract, Doug Utley's nice colt. I felt absolutely drained as we headed down to the winner's circle.

Despite my confidence in Stanley's ability, I had agonized over all the less-than-favorable outcomes of the race, knowing Stanley's penchant for getting into trouble. It was such a relief to have this race behind us.

Casual Lies learned a lot that afternoon, most of it positive. Chance felt Stanley had not only run greenly, but was trying to bully the other horses as he came to them. He added that Stanley was finally looking down the track toward the end, but he still didn't feel he'd ever really put much effort into the race.

Later that afternoon, when I was coming out of the racing office, a young man, obviously a jockey, asked me if I would take $75,000 for Casual Lies. I didn't know him and I still don't know who he was. I did, however, thank him as I turned him down. This would be the first of several offers that would come my way as time went on.

Chance also rode Stanley in his next race, the Mid-Peninsula Stakes at the Bay Meadows Fair, where Stanley ran a very mediocre race. The gate crew let me know that Stanley had acted pretty ornery in the gate and was playing with his tongue incessantly, getting it over the bit. Added to that information, Chance had heard Stanley making a gurgling sound while running around the turn. Putting the two reports together, I knew exactly what had gone wrong.

Casual Lies had swallowed his tongue, a racing expression for the tongue blocking a considerable part of a horse's air passage. From then on, we tied his tongue down to his bottom jaw. Stanley wasn't particularly fond of the tongue tie and tried endlessly to slide his tongue out of the specially made leather strap.

As a result, once a race had started, Stanley's tongue could usually be seen hanging out the side of his mouth all the way to the finish line. My stakes horse looked pretty silly running down the lane with his tongue flapping in the wind. He resembled a dog with his head hanging out of the car window. Better out than in, I said.

Shortly after that race Chance Rollins returned to Phoenix for the racing season at Turf Paradise. Thus, once again I found myself in need of a rider. When the agent for leading rider Russell Baze failed to return my call, the snub didn't surprise me.

For so many years, Jim had ridden all my horses. He was talented and savvy, and when he jumped off after riding in a race, the information and insight he brought back were invaluable in my training regimen. It was truly uncanny how accurately he could gauge the talent level of even the unraced horses. Unfortunately Jim was now 10 pounds too heavy to ride Thoroughbreds, and when he retired from race riding, it was problematic getting my first-choice jockey since most had prior commitments to the trainers they had been riding for.

After several jockey agents turned me down out of hand, Jim suggested that Alan Patterson ride Casual Lies for the next few races. Alan was a very nice man and a very competent rider who rode enough races to stay fit and keep his edge, and that suited me.

Besides, Stanley didn't care who rode him. A slave to his stomach as he continued to grow, Stanley's greatest concern was about who filled his feed tub.

Chapter Five

Let the Games Begin

Three weeks had passed since Casual Lies' desultory and extremely disappointing race in the Mid-Peninsula Stakes. He was now definitely full of himself and more than ready to run again.

He'd been training forwardly in his new tongue tie, so I was confident there wouldn't be a repeat of the gagging incident. What I couldn't predict was how anxious Stanley might be the next time he ran. Horses have long memories, and struggling to breathe while being bounced around in a full field of horses wouldn't have been very positive for Stanley's psyche. If he started to dread racing, and began to act out again, it wouldn't bode well for his future.

In fact, he needed to get a big boost from his next outing, and I found what I felt would be a good race for giving him just that: a six-furlong conditioned allowance race on September 18 at Bay Meadows, a non-winners of two and roughly four weeks after the Mid-Peninsula. He shouldn't have to expend much energy to win, because it would be an easy race for a horse of Stanley's quality. I definitely wanted this race to be a confidence-builder, for all concerned.

A non-winners of two is exactly that—none of the eligible horses entered has won two races. Keep in mind, a horse entered in a non-winners of two could've run 10 second-place finishes in a row prior to the race, and those 10 seconds could've been in stakes races. Entering a race with conditions didn't necessarily mean a walkover.

Racing secretaries put conditions on races to keep them competitive and thus interesting for the fans. Conditions also effectively keep the same horses from winning all the races in any particular category.

Handicapping with a negative bias, from the racing secretary to the race-going public, more weight was given to a horse's connections than to his past performances. I definitely attracted little or no attention as a trainer, and I used my flying under the industry's radar as a positive tool in my arsenal.

I could run the majority of my horses in cheaper races than where they probably belonged and with very little likelihood of a claim being dropped. Another nice caveat—I got better odds at the betting window and a chance to win easy purse money. Going about doing my business in a no-pressure atmosphere, answering to no one, unseen and unknown, were their own rewards.

Therefore it wasn't surprising when the morning line odds on Casual Lies suggested he would run last or next to last in the soft non-winners-of-two race. Fabulous! The rules of racing dictate that trainers can only bet on the horses they are saddling in a race and then only to win—this helps to discourage cheating. I bet Stanley to win, so the bigger the odds the better, as far as I was concerned. I seldom bet the horses, but I enjoyed a small flutter at the pari-mutuel window, particularly when I felt that the odds were ridiculously high on one of the horses I had entered.

At nearly 10-1 when the gate opened, Casual Lies settled into third, and it felt like he pretty much galloped for the entire six-furlong distance. When Stanley took the lead down the lane, jockey Alan Patterson had him under a strong hold. After the easy victory, Alan dismounted and confided: "Your horse felt like a million dollars, the power was amazing and I never had to ask him to run."

I laughed and said, "So you think you might want to ride him again?"

Alan rolled his eyes: "Oh, yeah!"

It was obvious Stanley wasn't suffering from a lack of confidence. He was fine. In fact Stanley had pulled up like a dynamo. As we say in the industry, "he was on the muscle."

The next morning after the race, he charged out of his stall, coiled up and practically walking on his tiptoes. He reminded me of a rodeo bull busting out of a chute, looking for a funny-faced guy in baggy pants. Being flatfooted around Stanley wasn't a particularly good idea at any time, but now more than ever we needed to be alert.

What with his pulling up so well from his race, I was eager to search for Casual Lies' next contest. The most obvious choice was the Foster City Mile running on October 28. With a little more than three weeks between races, the timing was perfect.

Not surprisingly, the handicappers and the betting public once again dismissed Casual Lies, sending him off at nearly 9-1. I legged Alan up on Stanley and hustled over to bet my money. Breaking well, Stanley settled into second, leaving very little daylight between him and Material Eyes, the early leader.

I had instructed Alan to bring Casual Lies from off the pace, laying maybe third or fourth in the seven horse field. Stanley had his own ideas about how he should run. While he wasn't running out of control, he was pulling hard with every stride. Alan, his feet way up in the dashboard, couldn't ease Stanley further off the pace without a real tussle. Fresh and enthusiastic, Stanley wasn't going to be denied.

Casual Lies reeled in the leader midway around the turn and engaged Material Eyes in a head-and-head battle from the top of the stretch to the wire. Striding as one, they were halfway down the lane and Stanley still hadn't opened up. I began to worry. Was he fit enough to go a mile?

I was hollering encouragement as if Stanley could hear it, when Jim shouted at me, "Alan hasn't let him run yet."

At the wire, Casual Lies poked his head in front, and he paid nearly $20 to win. Prior to entering the winner's circle, Alan was jubilant. I could hear him telling Jim how Stanley had been toying with the other horse.

"Did he interfere with him?" I asked Alan. Still very fresh in my memory was Stanley's first race, where Stanley had intimidated the other horses in the field.

"No, he was just so full of himself from the beginning, and when I eased him up to the other horse, he seemed content to go with him," Alan replied. "I knew he was going to win going down the backstretch. He was pulling, but he wasn't uncontrollable and it didn't take anything out of him. He's just such an incredibly strong two-year-old."

~

IT WAS SHORTLY AFTER STANLEY won the Foster City Mile that I got a telephone call from Duane Offield, a longtime friend and very successful Northern California trainer. I was still at the barn, finishing up with the morning chores when I answered. Following a few congratulations and some small talk, Duane asked me if I would sell Casual Lies. Not totally surprised by the question, I responded how Stanley had been for sale since the first day I'd bought him—for the right price, that is. Of course, with each race he won, that right price continued an upward spiral.

Duane offered me $265,000, a lot of money and a fair price in my mind. Though I hesitated—the prospect of losing Stanley made me feel horrible—when the call ended, I had accepted his offer. It was a Friday afternoon, and Duane was going to be spending the weekend with his clients. He said he would call me with the final details on Monday.

Jim was not pleased. He told me we would really regret selling Stanley now that he was just coming into his own. I already did, but I reminded him I had only adhered to our agreement—if anybody ever offered enough to pay off our house, we would accept the offer. But Jim wouldn't back down. He was adamant that we were making a huge mistake. Jim felt that Casual Lies was not just any horse; he was a world-class horse. I understood that. I felt the same way.

"But I already accepted his offer," I said. "I can't go back on my word."

When we arrived home, my mother, Helen, was visiting. She piped in with her opinion: If selling the horse wasn't going to make us happy, then we shouldn't do it; life was too short. Common sense was one of Mom's greatest gifts—and she had a way of clarifying any situation with only a few words.

"Change your mind," she said flatly.

Feeling miserable, Jim and I spent the longest weekend of our lives. I had sold a horse neither one of us wanted to lose.

Fate intervened once again. Monday came and went without a call from Duane. Casual Lies was still meant to be mine, and the relief around our shedrow was palpable for so many reasons. Common sense aside, at some point a colt that had been bought as a commodity in a business plan had morphed into something entirely different. Hopes, dreams and aspirations get very tangled in the world of horse racing. What looks fairly straightforward and as simple as winning or losing becomes secondary to the possibility of what could be.

My pinhooking business plan had not included still owning a horse at the point where he showed this much talent. Musing about "when we get the big horse" had become, "all right, we have the big horse; what do we do now?" To put it succinctly, we needed to fully explore our opportunities and let our aspirations take wing while trying to avoid the same exhilaration that caused Icarus to fly too close to the sun.

~

THE GRADE I HOLLYWOOD FUTURITY, now called the CashCall Futurity, appealed to any trainer with a nice two-year-old, especially one training in California. Held at Hollywood Park in Southern California, with a purse of $500,000, the Futurity was recognized as one of the premier two-year-old races in the entire country. Unbeknownst to me, it was also considered a prep race for the Kentucky Derby.

The 1991 running of the Hollywood Futurity would be on December 22, and I had nominated Casual Lies for it earlier in the year when the nomination fee was very cheap. It had seemed like a good investment as I grew to know just how special my fuzzy yearling was turning out to be.

Was I reaching a little too far? Maybe I was, but Stanley had been running so well. Three easy wins out of four races demonstrated he was very talented and strongly suggested he had the ability to take on tougher company. I found myself asking: "Why shouldn't I consider it? Because I would be criticized?" I certainly wasn't unfamiliar with criticism. Therefore, I embraced the potential and aimed my focus on the race I had always dreamed about winning. I started planning Stanley's training accordingly and began dreaming of a Futurity victory as the best Christmas present ever.

Being a realist, however, I knew Stanley would definitely

need another race prior to the Futurity. The problem was finding one he was eligible for that had 1) the right distance and 2) the right date for our schedule. Additionally, if we were going to have a fighting chance in the Futurity, we would need a prep race against two-year-olds having nearly the same ability as the ones we would face in a Grade I event.

Although Stanley's breeding indicated a distance of ground would suit him perfectly, getting him fit enough to run longer distances against much tougher company wouldn't be easy. After spending half his life scrawny, he had beefed up to become a bit of a chunky monkey. He was a good doer who loved his chow, licking and rattling the feed tub long after it was empty, at which point the begging began—annoying, relentless and extremely abrasive begging.

I couldn't shave a few pounds off him by cutting back on his food because he was still growing and needed a balanced feeding program. Besides, I was already giving him less food than most of the other horses in my barn.

I felt a good prep race could tighten him up to the level of fitness needed for the challenging race that was our ultimate goal. We would truly be hitting nosebleed atmosphere when it came to the quality of horses running in the Futurity and were pretty sure fitness would not be an issue for any of them.

Stanley's bloodlines gave promise of his running well on the turf, and this opened up several additional prep-race possibilities at Bay Meadows. Unfortunately, either the distances weren't right or the timing was too close to the Futurity. Plus they might not have offered the competitive level I sought. Therefore, I decided to enter Casual Lies in the Grade III Hoist the Flag Stakes going a mile and a sixteenth on the turf at Hollywood Park on the first day of December.

We shipped to Hollywood Park and quietly went about our business. We worked Stanley on the turf, but we couldn't get a feel for how he was going to run on it. It was pretty apparent that the turf—despite his breeding—wasn't going to move him up. But we had made the decision, and we didn't have time to find another suitable race.

Casual Lies broke third from post position three in the Hoist the Flag and galloped along in fourth until he belatedly made a move on the final turn. As he edged up into third on the outside, he looked strong and well placed for the run down the lane. Unfortunately, he went straight when he should have hugged the turn, sacrificing many lengths to his competition. Once he straightened out, however, he made back some of the ground he had lost and finished fourth.

Alan who had flown down to ride Stanley in the race, explained the colt hadn't handled the turf well at all. When I asked him why he had run straight instead of taking the turn, Alan said Stanley had tried to jump something and it threw him off stride.

Although we returned home disappointed, I still wanted to run Stanley in the Futurity. Undeniably he was getting valuable experience and improving his fitness with each race. I didn't feel we should deny him—or us—a chance at the Futurity based on his fourth-place finish in the Hoist the Flag, a surface that obviously confused him. Plus Stanley was still a very young two-year-old compared to a lot of his competition. In some cases, he was spotting them many months of maturity.

~

WHEN WE HEADED SOUTH AGAIN, this time for the Hollywood Futurity, I knew I was asking a lot of my horse. But at the same time, I knew as a lightly raced colt with a very promising future he had a lot more in the tank.

The Hoist the Flag race conditions required Stanley to carry top weight of 121 pounds, seven pounds more than any of the horses who'd finished in front of him. That's a lot of weight for a two-year-old to give to his opposition. The only other horse to carry the same high weight of 121 pounds was the favorite, who'd finished next to last in that race. By contrast, all the horses would carry the same weight in the Hollywood Futurity.

For the most part, our time at Hollywood Park was a pretty quiet time, and we traveled about with a certain amount of anonymity. It didn't take long to train one horse, and if you hung around the barn afterward, Stanley wouldn't settle down. Most mornings we wandered over to the track and watched the horses exercise while enjoying the atmosphere of a major race meet.

The route from our barn to the track led us past a stable with a huge snow-white goose. This pugnacious critter spent his morning stalking two-legged interlopers who violated what he perceived as his personal territory. I frequently laughed heartily when well-heeled, unsuspecting owners suddenly broke into a high-stepping run with this obstreperous goose hot on their heels, hissing at full volume, wings flapping, while pecking them in the butt.

The animal's antics amused me until one morning I rounded a corner and found he had spotted me. He rushed at me with his wings spread and in a full-throated hiss. Caught in the moment, I looked around and saw quite an audience waiting for me to turn and run. I was just another character in that morning's enactment of "Who's Getting Goosed Today?"

I wasn't about to let all those people laugh as I made a run for it. Heaven forbid if the press was to hear about what could only be a thoroughly undignified incident. I could imagine the headlines.

I stood my ground and prepared to take my pecking. The goose stopped in front of me. He was huge with his neck arched like a cobra and wings spread wide. He bent over and slowly stuck his head between my knees, hissing the whole while.

"Nope, do your best; I'm not running away," I hissed back.

After a moment or two he gave up, stalked away, and the disappointed crowd dispersed. Apparently, Goose Boy preferred the chase to the standoff. For my part, no longer amused, I felt the better part of valor would be to take a different route from our barn to the racetrack in the future.

As the big race approached, the handicappers weren't giving us any chance at all. But then again, they spent very little ink reporting on our appearance in the race. Ignored rather than overlooked didn't matter. It smelled the same.

When the day of the Hollywood Futurity arrived, quite a crowd gathered at the saddling paddock. I thought my horse, physically at least, didn't seem all that out of place. His race record certainly outshone several of the horses in the race, though it was definitely not as good as some of the others.

The crowd's attention focused on a very fine-boned and feminine-looking horse. As it turned out this was the $2.9 million sales yearling A. P. Indy. He had sold the same year as Casual Lies, also at Keeneland but in the selected yearlings edition.

A few of the other trainers took a good look at Casual Lies as he paraded around the tree-studded saddling paddock, but they weren't talking to me. While this was going on, I was looking as closely at their horses as they looked at mine. Stanley somehow seemed bigger than most of them—if not in height, definitely in bulk. Though sleek and shiny, Stanley didn't have the well-honed lines and definition of the majority of the horses in this race.

When the gate opened and the field was away in the Futurity, we held steady in fifth position. Within a quarter of mile, Casual Lies with Alan aboard was laying third and very quickly moved into second place. He remained there, pressing the pace but not under a pull. I couldn't help wondering why we were once again pressing the pace. I would have preferred to see him farther back in the pack, saving something for the drive down the lane.

Despite his position Stanley was still running well against top-notch horses. These tactics helped to set up the brilliant finish of A.P. Indy, who ultimately beat Dance Floor by a neck. When it looked liked the field was going to swallow Stanley up on the final turn and he was dropping from second to fourth, our colt dug down and found more. He not only ran on to finish third for himself, he did it by a full two lengths in front of the remainder of the field. In his call of the finish, the track announcer characterized the effort as "a great job by Casual Lies."

I have watched the replay of that race so many times, and with each watching I continue to be astounded by the move Stanley made at the head of the lane. Granted, the first and second finishers pulled away, winning and placing easily. But to get swallowed up by the rest of the field after pressing the pace, only to come back on and open up two lengths on the remainder of the field—this was a very brave move for a two-year-old who had spent the majority of the race near the front end. He was definitely the best of the rest that day. The two horses he'd dueled with for the lead finished behind him.

My cheap little $7,500 yearling, the one that nobody really wanted, had just earned nearly $90,000 for that third-place finish, and at odds of 52-1. I wasn't in the habit of entering horses to run for third, but I was proud and thrilled at how game my colt had run. No race in Northern California for two-year-olds would have paid that much money to the winner, let alone for third. Besides, and even more important, we were now Grade I stakes-placed.

Horses who have won or placed in races of this quality and importance have earned the distinction of being competitive with the very best of the best, and winning or placing in a graded stakes race is a crowning achievement for a stallion prospect. Select stake races are graded from I to III, and several criteria must be met for each coveted designation. The most important are the purse size and the quality of the horses that run in the race from year to year. If a race fails to attract the right kind of horses, it will eventually be either downgraded or lose its designation entirely.

The Grade I Hollywood Futurity was the last race Casual Lies would run in as a two-year-old. With three wins and one third out of six starts, he had total earnings of more than $150,000. I couldn't have been more thrilled—or so I thought at the time. Fate wasn't done with us, however, not by a long shot.

Chapter Six

Three-Year-Olds and Derbies

With the Hollywood Futurity behind us, I had my eye firmly set on the Grade III El Camino Real Derby at Bay Meadows in San Mateo. With the race scheduled to be run a little more than four weeks after the Futurity, the timing couldn't have been better for Stanley's next race.

Coming home to Northern California and training in familiar territory was a pleasant relief for the entire team. I felt confident my horse would make a good showing in the Bay Meadows stakes race, even though no horse based in Northern California had ever won the El Camino Real Derby and its juicy $300,000 purse up to that point in time.

With the arrival of January 1st, Stanley was now officially a three-year-old who had closed out his two-year-old season by running at Hollywood Park in two stakes races, extremely challenging races that gave him more experience and made him a good deal fitter. I couldn't fault my colt for failing to win either of those two races in Southern California. However, his pressing the early leaders in the last race drove home the point that Casual Lies would fare better coming from off the pace.

This wasn't exactly an epiphany since taking him off the early pace had been my objective for several races. Sure, Stanley had speed—plenty of speed actually. However, Stanley's burst of speed only lasted for about five-sixteenths of a mile, and then he would flatten out.

We could use that burst of speed at the beginning of the

race, on the turn or where it really counted—down the lane. I chose down the lane, where 55 percent of the purse money awaited the first horse to cross the finish line.

Since the El Camino Real Derby was going to be another tough race, getting weight off Stanley became a priority. He would run better and farther if he wasn't packing so much weight. I couldn't take any more grain away from him. I had long since taken oat hay off his menu, and he was down to little more than a whisper of alfalfa in the evening, his favorite treat. For some time I'd been stuffing his feedbag with timothy hay—expensive but not fattening. Stanley didn't particularly like it, however. Pulling the timothy out of the hay bag, looking for something tastier, he used it for bedding.

Because Stanley was running regularly and training forwardly in between his races, I had to ask myself—how was he continuing to hold so much weight? Turns out he was eating the straw used for bedding his stall. Most horses will do a little nibbling on the straw but not to any great degree. The more I limited Stanley's rations, the more he compensated by eating his bedding. We couldn't believe how little straw was left when we cleaned his stall in the morning. Talk about a midnight snacker. Did the little devil ever sleep?

Empty calories with basically no nutritional value, straw will hold weight on a horse who consumes large amounts. Our solution? Rice hulls. We cleared his stall of every last shred of straw and replaced it with the rice hulls, the husks removed from the rice seed. Horses get bored with those rather quickly, eating only a few mouthfuls. Rice hulls were far cleaner and safer for my horse, holding up much better than my other option, which would have been wood shavings, while producing less dust.

When I led Stanley back into his stall, he was delighted to

sink ankle deep into what must have looked like, at least to him, a bed of whole oats. Impatiently, he waited for me to remove his halter so that he could feast ravenously upon the unexpected bounty.

After cramming his mouth full, he almost immediately started spitting it out. Obviously thunderstruck, he pawed and stomped about, throwing his version of an equine tantrum. This cranky behavior persisted for the next several days. Stanley was furious his 24-hour, all-you-can eat buffet had been shut down.

Within a week of taking the straw off the menu, we could clearly see a change. The muscle definition of a horse both strong and fit began to emerge.

~

STANLEY HAD BOUNCED BACK from our time in Southern California with his usual zest for life, his eyes glowed with anticipation, and he was full of mischief. We had to be careful to give his stall a very wide berth. Desperate to drag me over to his stall, he would snake his head out, grabbing at my clothing as I walked by. He flirted incessantly, begging for attention.

Stanley wasn't the type of horse you could put behind a full stall screen and leave to his own devices. Without all the socializing he required, I think Stanley could have become very aggressive and nasty out of sheer frustration. My small, more personalized operation perfectly suited his needy personality and helped him flourish. Naturally, I was criticized, accused of spoiling Casual Lies outrageously and treating him as if he were a pet rather than a star athlete. Frankly I didn't see why he couldn't be both—it's what we both wanted.

Days off didn't set well with Stanley, and walking him by

hand was an exercise in horsemanship as well as endurance. Bouncing off the walls, he didn't need a lot of training, but he did require a lot of my focus. Stanley's next race couldn't come about fast enough for him.

~

NOT TOO LONG AFTER OUR return from Hollywood Park, the phone rang. It was Duane Offield, only this time it wasn't about buying Casual Lies. Duane wasted little time coming to the point of his call when he asked me if I had nominated Casual Lies to the Triple Crown.

After I stopped laughing, I said succinctly, "Yeah, right! Duane, we ran a distant third in the Hollywood Futurity, a long ways from winning it." To say Duane didn't care much for my response would have been an understatement.

"What's wrong with you?" he asked me. "You have a great horse. Why wouldn't you spend $600 for an early bird nomination?"

"Duane, it's not about the nomination fee. I know he's a great horse. No one is a more loyal rider of the Casual Lies bandwagon than me. I have been passing up much easier racing to run him in the type of races that I think he deserves to run in. Unfortunately, the difference between Triple Crown racing and the level of competition we have been taking on represents another whole universe of racing."

"A supplemental late fee to enter the Kentucky Derby *alone* is a huge amount." Duane said. "What's another $600 in the scheme of things? Nominating him now gives you the option to consider running him in the Triple Crown after he wins his next race. If for no other reason, do it for Stanley!"

Bingo. With that last comment, Duane had pushed the right button.

"I'll think about it," I finally said.

"Don't think for long," he replied. "The early bird nominations close in the next few days. I'll send the form over today."

Duane was as good as his word. The form arrived that very evening at feeding time. I looked it over with trepidation and, feeling decidedly foolish, ultimately filled it in and sent it off. It still makes my heart skip a beat when I remember looking at the very imposing Triple Crown nomination form. For the first time I was forced to seriously consider what filling out and sending in a nomination to the Triple Crown really meant.

Emotionally complicated, it seemed like I was reaching for a star I couldn't see. Shelley Riley, the owner and trainer of a Triple Crown contender—the very thought had the hallucinatory quality of a delusionary vision.

Duane's timely intervention was just another example of how rigid a course fate had set for me. If Duane had failed to get involved at exactly the right time, I wouldn't have nominated Casual Lies for the Triple Crown, and I would have still been wondering twenty years later what might have been.

As an obscure woman in a male-dominated profession, I certainly wouldn't be popping off about running my horse in the Kentucky Derby. The deluge of criticism would be monumental, and I didn't relish the thought of being the brunt of unkind jokes. I was already dubbed the "Horsewise Housewife," a pithy comment making the rounds.

~

I PUT THOUGHTS OF THE Triple Crown on the back burner as we focused our energy on the El Camino Real Derby. Despite his third in the Hollywood Futurity, Casual Lies went off as the bettors' fourth choice in the race. I had instructed Alan

Patterson to lay off the leaders and let Casual Lies do his running down the lane.

Breaking from the sixth post position, Casual Lies was well placed in fourth before a quarter of a mile had elapsed. Pulling strongly, Stanley was extremely fresh and wasn't going to be denied for long, moving easily into the lead after three quarters of a mile. At the top of the lane, Casual Lies opened up and went on to win the El Camino Real Derby by a half-length.

Staying off the early pace, along with a big reduction in body fat, had worked beautifully. Our share of the purse? $165,000.

Standing in the winner's circle with a dazed look on my face, I realized this was another turning point for me. Casual Lies wasn't just any horse that came along with a few wins in the tank. This colt was going to be world class; he was now a *graded stakes winner*.

As I turned to follow my colt back to the barn area, a man appeared from the crowd of well wishers to inform me there was a scheduled press conference for the winning trainer. I hesitated, looking over my shoulder as my horse walked away with Jim. I was torn because I make it a habit to watch my horses cool out. You can learn a great deal about how they have pulled up after their races by being there for the whole test-barn process.

When a race concludes, the winner is always tested for illegal substances, along with one or two other horses from the race. You get a free bath, and you walk your horse until he has drunk his fill. Once he has cooled out sufficiently and needs to urinate, a test-barn official will take him into a stall, close the top and bottom door and wait patiently for the horse to do its business, catching a sample in a specially designed container. The state veterinarian is also there to take a blood sample, testing for substance levels as well as anything that might not be detected in the urine sample.

Over the years I have found horses that have trouble cooling out could be percolating a problem, even though there are no overt signs. If you're observant, you can see even the most subtle differences in your horse, and those differences you observe can put you ahead of the curve in your training program. Generally, horses having trouble at the test barn are either dragging around or they simply can't seem to settle down—and of course, I desperately wanted to be there to see how Stanley was doing.

However, the unexpected press conference was something I felt obligated to attend. I would count on Jim to give me the test-barn information I needed on Stanley.

Obediently following along, I was led through the excited crowd and into the corporate offices to the room designated for the press conference. I was seated at the head of what appeared to be a boardroom conference table, and there must have been 10 or 12 reporters waiting for me to arrive. I had never heard of anything like this for a local race, but then, I certainly didn't have any personal experience with winning a race of this importance.

In the blink of an eye, they were firing questions at me. I was flabbergasted and entirely too excited to remember much of what was said. But I do recall for the most part they seemed less surprised that Casual Lies had won the El Camino Real Derby than they were stunned Shelley Riley was the trainer of the winner of the El Camino Real Derby. The majority of the questions centered on me and how I felt, rather than on what was next for Casual Lies.

I survived my first press conference, and I can't say that I didn't enjoy it. I was sky high on a jug full of happy after winning such a prestigious race with the horse I cared so much about. When Jim and I finally arrived home that evening, the answering machine in the kitchen was blinking red. It took nearly 20 minutes to hear all the messages played out. The best was from Ron and Rexanne Hawkins, who were so gleeful they sounded like they'd shared their own big jug of happy, probably at least 34 proof from the sounds of it.

Together Jim and I stood in the kitchen, exhausted yet still able and willing to smile and laugh along with the voices of our friends. It was difficult to let go of the day and unwind sufficiently to go to bed that night. Once there I found myself dreaming, but I wasn't asleep.

~

THE PHONE NOT ONLY RANG every morning for days on end after the race. It rang all day long and sometimes late into the evening. My anonymity had evaporated, along with anything remotely resembling the quiet life I was accustomed to.

The local racing media still wasn't prepared to embrace Casual Lies wholeheartedly, and they certainly weren't suggesting his destiny might include running in the Kentucky Derby. They were interested, however, in reporting on anything that had to do with him—more specifically, me.

Somewhere along the way, it had been discovered I had nominated Casual Lies to the Triple Crown. Whispered rumors abounded not only about the Kentucky Derby, but the possibility I would be selling my horse long before that event ever took place. The reporters weren't shy about asking for confirmation, either. "Was I selling my dream?" "Who was interested in buying Casual Lies?" "Why wouldn't I sell Casual Lies?" "Where was I running him next?" "Why would I ever consider running Casual Lies in the Kentucky Derby?"

My personal favorites were: "Why, with all the choices

available in the local jockey colony, had I chosen Alan Patterson to ride Casual Lies?" "Would I consider sending Casual Lies to a trainer with more experience?" You've really got to love that last question.

The racing public, however, was gung ho. They smelled a local hero, and they were ready to embrace the dream—and that is exactly what happened. We all got caught up in the impossible dream. After all, where was the harm?

Suddenly the thought of participating in the Run for the Roses didn't seem quite so ridiculous, and I found myself flirting with the possibility. I would need to step carefully going forward, knowing each decision I made could have monumental consequences.

If somewhat tentatively, I began to include the Kentucky Derby in our future plans, even though I knew a harsh reality was always one step away if it were a bad step taken by Casual Lies or a high temperature and a lingering upper respiratory infection. Within the bounds of possibility, we had found our wings, and we were flying high on an updraft fueled by our current success.

Casual Lies pulled up after his race as if he had run in a non-winners of two rather than a tough graded stakes race. I tried to rest Casual Lies as much as he was willing to put up with. Then I started marching him toward his next contest, the Sausalito Stakes at Golden Gate Fields, which would run roughly six weeks after the El Camino Real.

Golden Gate Fields rests on the edge of the San Francisco Bay, and its racing surface was definitely on the sandy side. Some horses loved it, while others hated it, and I wanted to have some idea how Stanley would handle the track before I committed to the Sausalito Stakes. Therefore, as we neared the entry date for the race, the decision was made to give Stanley his last pre-race workout at Golden Gate Fields.

To that end, I called the racing office to arrange for a stall we could use on the morning we planned to work Stanley. They responded like I had just announced the imminent arrival of the President of the United States. They directed me to bring my rig to the back gate, allowing me closer access to the stakes barn, and they assured me a stall would be readied for my horse.

When we pulled up to the normally padlocked gate on the morning of the workout, a security guard was waiting to run interference for us, and it turned out to be a godsend. Apparently the racing office had announced Casual Lies was coming to town, because a gang of photographers and reporters had showed up to follow our every move.

As we unloaded Casual Lies, Brownie and our gear, we were the object of a tremendous amount of curiosity. Oh my god, I thought, what if Stanley worked badly in front of all these people?

When we approached the track, Jim on Brownie and Alan Patterson on Stanley, trainers, jockeys, grooms, pony people and even racing board personnel lined the rail. I was horrified. Turn the screws a little tighter. This was more nerve-wracking than watching him run in the afternoon. These were my peers lining the rail—I couldn't help but want Stanley to make a good impression for my sake as well as his.

My stakes-winning colt was the opposite side of the coin—he loved it. He stood at the entrance of the racetrack gazing alertly off into infinity, posing. You weren't going to hurry Stanley along when he had an adoring crowd to admire him. What a ham.

Striding beautifully, Stanley worked well, looking powerful and well within himself. The media, who had chased us to the track, chased us back to the barn. It was like we had our very own entourage.

86

The reporters were friendly as they began to ask me questions. I was used to being ignored, and when asked about my horses, I tended to be introspective. I didn't want to sound overly confident. Despite the confidence I had in my horse, too many things happen in horse racing to guarantee a sure thing.

Even though I am gregarious by nature, I could at times be very self-conscious. It wasn't going to be easy to bare my soul to the press. After all, I knew a great deal of what I said to them would end up in print. While I didn't refuse to answer their questions, I was afraid of talking myself into a position of being ridiculed or second-guessed—and this made me very cautious with them.

Almost immediately the tenor of their questions maneuvered me into defending the confidence I had in my horse. It was pointed out the horses we had outrun in the El Camino Real Derby weren't really much more than second stringers, at least as far as they were concerned.

Oh brother—disparaging me was one thing; picking on Stanley was another. A few reporters had built up the glass-slipper aspect of Stanley's success, but the more popular trend was the Ma and Pa Kettle scenario: "How did you get a horse like this? What's the best horse you ever trained? What makes you think you have enough experience to train a horse like this? What are you going to do with all that money?"

I had never felt such pressure, and it wasn't fun. Suddenly, everything I said or did with regard to Casual Lies became news. The handicappers on the other hand were having a great time voicing the opinion that Casual Lies would get beat in the Sausalito Stakes.

When race day arrived, so many cameramen hustled into the saddling paddock that it was hard to get around. The huge crowd of racing fans pressed tightly to the glass partitions separating the saddling paddock from the lower level of the grandstand. There was a constant tapping on the glass as people called out to attract my attention and wish me luck.

This all made winning seem even more important than it already was, taking some of the fun away. On the other hand, the public was having a ball; they made Casual Lies a runaway favorite. This added more pressure because nothing seems worse than a disappointed crowd when a heavy favorite gets beat. I didn't think it was likely or even possible for Stanley to get beat on that day, but then again, the one sure thing in horse racing is the uncertainty.

Once Casual Lies was handed off to the pony person accompanying him through the warm-up to the starting gate, Jim and I beat a hasty retreat to the owners' boxes. I sat there out of breath, listening to the sound of my heart pounding in my ears as I waited for the race to commence. I glanced down toward the saddling paddock and directly into two of the most enormous camera lenses I had ever seen. Almost instantly my nose began to itch unbearably. Was there no place I could hide?

As the horses approached the gate, I wondered if I was going to have a heart attack. My heart pounded so hard that it was painful, and my left arm began to tingle alarmingly. In retrospect, I suspect it was a controlled panic attack. I just wanted the race to be over, with my horse safe, sound and back at my barn.

Stanley stumbled badly coming out of the gate, and I surged to my feet, aghast. Knowing him, he was probably screwing around when the gate opened. He recovered quickly and, within a few jumps, was stalking the leaders. After three-quarters of a mile, Stanley had the lead and went on to win ever so easily. The crowd was screaming, joyous in their celebration, and it was very difficult to get back down to the track through all the well wishers. We still had to get through the winner's circle photo and the trophy presentation. Heaven help the reporters—I was on the run and wouldn't be talking to them anytime soon.

I didn't learn until later that Casual Lies had just run the mile and a sixteenth in the fastest time for a three-year-old, at least to that point in the current season, in the entire United States. Obviously, Stanley did indeed like the sandy going over the Golden Gate track.

Frankly, I was just glad the race was over. The pressure leading up to it had been nearly unbearable for me. My horse was doing great—I was the one who needed to find a way to deal with the increasingly bright spotlight being focused on me by the media.

Then there were the very real expectations of the Bay Area racing fans. Their growing interest in me and my horse was adding tenfold to the tension I was feeling. Casual Lies didn't know anything had changed. He was just doing what he loved to do, and that was run like crazy. He knew how to get revved up. It was my job to be a steady influence on him so he wouldn't get himself hurt, while at the same time heaping on the love and attention he craved.

With Stanley winning impressively twice in a row, I expected the scrutiny on him and me to intensify more than ever before, and boy, did it ever. Compared to what the future held for us, however, this was just the calm before the storm.

Chapter Seven

Pick Me – Pick Me – No, No, Pick Me!

After Casual Lies' impressive win in the Sausalito Stakes, the local television stations were clamoring for interviews. Coming to quiet Pleasanton in the afternoon, their mobile rigs attracted attention like a bright light attracts moths. I had never seen a satellite truck set up in the Pleasanton barn area to interview anyone, let alone me.

Although Bay-area broadcasting coverage rarely included horse racing, the stations apparently felt Stanley's local-makes-good story would have broad appeal for their viewers.

Armed with warm and engaging smiles, interviewers typically asked the same questions: "How did you find this horse? What do you think the future holds for you and your horse? How does it feel to be the center of so much attention? Are you actually going to run Casual Lies in the Kentucky Derby?" While this was going on, Stanley would try ceaselessly to eat the microphones, pull bits of clothing off the interviewers, nibble at their faces or snuffle in their hair.

Interviews that included Casual Lies always turned into a wrestling match. As long as I owned Stanley, he never bit me in anger, or anyone else for that matter. However, if you weren't careful, he could pinch a nice little blood blister on you. On those occasions when he managed to sneak past your defenses and give you a nip, he was gone in a hurry before you could give him a swat. Stanley was being playful, but those little nips hurt like crazy.

Next to running and eating, tug of war was Stanley's

favorite pastime. If he got a piece of your clothing in his teeth, you were faced with the prospect of prying it out of his mouth while avoiding one of those painful nips. If you failed to free yourself, he would take off into the depths of his stall with a chunk of your clothing waving around like a flag. Can you imagine the evening news with my blouse being torn off? I cringed at the thought, to be sure.

If I tried leaving Stanley in his stall and stepping away for the interview, he'd fire up his favorite distraction routines— teeth scraping, bucking, snorting, squealing and peppering the walls with his hind hoofs. He could be such a brat. Either I had to distract Stanley by stepping over to him and subjecting myself to his playful mauling or take the chat into the tack room and shut the door.

Partly because the interviewers weren't practiced handicappers, they tended not to ask the kind of questions that would make me uncomfortable, like was I going to change riders or was I going to sell Casual Lies, among other queries. So it was fun going home to watch myself on the local news, even if I did occasionally get nipped on air.

Where I thought the phone was ringing off the hook before, now it became a constant background cacophony, adding a particularly annoying cadence to the otherwise pleasant shedrow harmony.

Increasing numbers of people were stopping by the barn daily just to take a look at me and Casual Lies. But frankly, I don't know how they were getting past the guards at the stable gate, especially if they weren't licensed horsemen. Quiet and countrified Alameda County Fairgrounds was becoming a curiosity seeker's paradise.

Stanley was not into dull and quiet, and because our barn had become anything but dull and quiet, he was overjoyed with all the sensory stimulation.

The source of that stimulation was becoming a problem, however. With several horses in training for regular clients, we had a racing stable to run. I preferred the hands-on approach to the daily care of my charges, doing most of the work myself along with Jim's help. My normal routine of attending to the morning chores in an orderly fashion was made nearly impossible by the sudden influx of sightseers.

For example, I would lead a tacked-up horse down the shedrow with Jim in the saddle and find a group of tourists in our path. Even worse was arriving back from the track to see a group gathered around Stanley's stall while one of the tourists was attempting to pull a piece of clothing out of his mouth. This was just not working out too well.

Thus, between the constant ringing of the phone and the tourists, I had to make changes in order to lessen the distraction. I installed an answering machine and put barricades around the entrances to the shedrow. The phone continued to ring, but now I could screen the calls.

The tourists continued to come, but for the most part they respected the barricades and stayed behind them. That didn't stop them from taking pictures or pointing and asking endless questions. People even brought gifts for Stanley, offering up bags of carrots and apples, much to his delight. They brought me articles they had clipped out of the papers, just in case I hadn't seen them.

As I rushed about trying to keep up with all the things that needed doing each day, I always took a moment to acknowledge their interest and well wishes. After all I couldn't be rude and ignore them entirely. This whole story was good for racing, and I was becoming, at the very least, a local ambassador for it. Thank goodness for Jim. He took up the slack, doing many of the things I would normally have been doing, and was fine with it. He didn't like talking to the press or the tourists.

Somewhere around this time, I got a call from a man who said he was representing Sid and Jenny Craig. He wanted to know if Casual Lies could be bought.

Uh-oh, I thought, and out loud replied, "For the right price."

"Would you consider $2.7 million?" he said.

I clutched the edge of my desk. After all, I joked later, I only gave $7.5 thousand for my colt.

He went on to say, "The arrangement would be $1.2 million up front, $700,000 after Casual Lies ran in the Kentucky Derby and the other $800,000 on a date to be determined. There would be two box seats to the Derby and a limo."

Oh brother, I thought, it's another fishing exhibition.

"What, no Sunday hat?" I responded.

Obviously, they didn't think much of my business acumen if they thought I would sell a living, breathing creature on the installment plan. Despite what they might have thought, I was no Minnie Pearl.

I have since read the following comment in an interview with Ron McAnally, trainer for the Craigs at the time: "We showed an interest in Casual Lies, but Shelley Riley wanted $3 million." I don't know where the difference between that $3 million and the $2.7 million inquiry I received came from—unless of course the agent was deducting a 10% commission for himself.

I do know I never turned down a legitimate offer for Casual Lies. My response to Sid and Jenny Craig's agent had been, "If I sold my horse, it would be for payment in full and only in one installment before the horse changed hands." After that I didn't hear anything further from this agent.

I don't know how the press found out about the offer, but

once they had, they sniffed after the story endlessly. Shelley Riley had turned down $2.7 million for Casual Lies. It didn't seem to matter how many times I told them—if a check had been pushed across the table for $2.7 million, I would have pushed the lead shank back.

Ultimately, I heard the Craig's had bought Dr Devious for $2.5 million from someone in England. I will now say with certainty, if Jenny Craig had called me on the phone and said she wanted to buy Casual Lies for her husband as a birthday present for $2.7 million, I would have said yes. Frankly, I doubt I would have turned down anything over $1.5 million, to be paid in one lump sum. But that was then, and looking back endlessly will only result in a stiff neck.

~

ONE CLEAR AND SPARKLING morning, shortly after the chores were done and the horses were nostril-deep into their midmorning grain allocation, I was settled in my office filling in the training charts. I was mulling over the mornings activities in my head and fine-tuning the training plan for each horse, making adjustments according to how they had trained that day. When the phone rang, I picked it up on the first ring, still engrossed in my task. That was the moment when Tom Knust introduced himself into my adventure.

Tom was the racing secretary at Santa Anita Park in Arcadia, just east of Los Angeles. Southern California racing had now officially recognized our team of three. Of course, the previous summer when I was looking for a stall for Casual Lies at the Del Mar racing meet, I had never received a callback from Tom or anyone else in the Del Mar racing office.

Tom was now calling to introduce me to the thought of running Casual Lies in the Santa Anita Derby. Still harboring a little resentment over the lack of response to my stall request, I wasn't particularly impressed. My plan was to run Casual Lies in the California Derby at Golden Gate Fields, a track he obviously loved. This was the race I planned to use as our Kentucky Derby prep, if we even went to Louisville, which was just an uncertain glimmer on the horizon. The California Derby would help answer any lingering questions I might still be harboring about the wisdom of such a lofty quest.

To get a call from the Santa Anita racing office was definitely a new experience for me. Infrequently over the years a racing secretary would call and ask me to help fill a race on the fair circuit, but this was completely different. This wasn't just about filling a race; it was about pulling in the public with a strong and interesting field. Santa Anita wanted a full field of the best three-year-olds available for their Derby.

Tom was very smooth and extremely good at his job. With his silky and honey-toned voice, he set about recruiting Casual Lies for the Santa Anita Derby, and he was relentless. At least once every morning, two of the many phone calls that came in would be from either Tom Knust or Bob Umphrey, Tom's counterpart at Golden Gate Fields.

I had already expressed my interest in running Casual Lies in the California Derby. Why Bob would call every morning was a mystery to me. In retrospect, I suppose he knew I would be getting calls from Santa Anita, so he put my number on speed dial to touch base with me daily. It was in Bob's best interest to be sure I followed through with my commitment to run Casual Lies in his Derby rather than in the more prestigious Santa Anita Derby.

So every morning I would hear, "Hi Shelley, how are you and Casual Lies this morning?" Bob never called Casual Lies

Stanley, and truthfully, the Casual Lies query was really the main purpose of his calls. Stanley's wellbeing was probably nearly as important to Bob as it was to me. Having Casual Lies on the card would be a huge draw, perhaps big enough to set a record attendance at Golden Gate Fields on California Derby day.

Then one evening at home, I answered the phone to find myself talking to Steven Ford, President Ford's son. His job was to recruit Casual Lies for the Jim Beam Stakes at Turfway Park in Kentucky. Whoa, that was so cool. I loved President Ford. I told Steven if he could get his father to present the trophy, I would give him my assurance that Casual Lies would be there, replete with colorful red, white and blue ribbons in his mane.

He laughed and went on to give me all the reasons why it would be in my best interest to run my horse in Kentucky, using the Jim Beam as his primary prep for the Kentucky Derby, a President Ford presentation aside. I countered by pointing out the obvious. It was a long way to travel when I still wasn't sure we were even going to go on to the Kentucky Derby. He parried with the argument that I would have the opportunity to run against some of the East Coast's best three-year-olds, some of whom would be Kentucky Derby contenders. Casual Lies would get a feel for the surfaces that we would encounter and have an opportunity to acclimate to the different weather. Plus when the race was over it would be an easy transfer to Louisville. Overall, it was basically the same pitch, different speaker.

Other racing secretaries called, from Canada to Florida and parts in between, but Santa Anita Park, Golden Gate Fields and Turfway Park were the big three for us and ultimately the only ones that we seriously considered. It was amazing, though, how many racing secretaries considered my horse good enough to invite to their parties. Tom, for his part, threw all of the considerable weight of Santa Anita at us to convince me to bring my horse to run in their race.

Tom had a great sense of humor and was practiced at lobbing each of my objections right back at me. He was highly effective at twisting everything to shed a favorable light on his suggestions, while at the same time being very adept at parrying my objections without offending me. He opined that there wasn't a better race in the country to find out if I really had a horse capable of competing in the Kentucky Derby. Hmmm. . . .Not only that, Tom was adamant that if I seriously wanted to have a chance of winning the Kentucky Derby, this was the race that Casual Lies should be running in. Double hmmm. . .

I wasn't convinced. The California Derby was the closest to a guaranteed win I was ever going to get in the always-uncertain world of horse racing. Tom pointed out that the Santa Anita Derby had a much bigger purse. I countered with why would I want to travel all the way to Santa Anita, only to run second or third while getting beat up by their local press? Naturally he came back with the answer to the most important question I had for myself: "To find out if Casual Lies could beat the kind of horses that would be running in the Kentucky Derby." While this was true, I still had to wonder why we would want to take on those horses before we had to, even though I knew my horse was still improving with each race.

After all, A.P. Indy had already beaten us, and although Bertrando had finished second in the Breeders' Cup two-year-old race, it had been to the amazing Arazi. Inasmuch as the trainers of A.P. Indy and Bertrando had already announced their intentions of running in the Santa Anita Derby, I was hard-pressed to find a single enticement for shipping Stanley to Southern California.

In my opinion, another local win under Stanley's belt would be much nicer than running him in a mini Kentucky Derby at Santa Anita. If Stanley didn't run well in his next race, whichever one I ultimately chose, he simply wouldn't be going to Kentucky. Being away from my barn for any length of time, as had been the case when we ran in the Hoist the Flag and the Hollywood Futurity, was proving very expensive, and all the safety factors for Stanley were already in place at Pleasanton. These were just a few of the arguments I espoused in the face of Tom's cajolery.

Sensing he wasn't making a lot of headway, Tom tried a new tack. He proposed Jim and I fly down and spend the day at the races as guests of Santa Anita. We could see Bertrando, one of the tougher opponents we would eventually face, run in the Grade II San Felipe Stakes. Tom went on to suggest he could easily arrange for us to talk to Charlie Whittingham. Perhaps that legendary trainer would have some advice that could help us with our decision-making.

Now that was a pretty hard offer to turn down. Tom was pleased when I accepted, and Santa Anita rolled out the red carpet.

Our five-star VIP trip to Santa Anita was quite an experience. It was like stepping straight into a Hollywood TV script. We arrived at the airport in Burbank to find a uniformed chauffeur waiting for our flight with a mile-long limo parked right outside the door of the concourse. And that was just the beginning to what would turn out to be a very glamorous afternoon.

As the limo glided to a stop in front of the Turf Club entrance, the door of the limo opened and we were greeted by name—pretty heady stuff for me. I surmised they must have circulated our photos to the staff. I'm sure the race goers who stopped to stare were surprised to see just who did, or maybe in this case who didn't, exit the stretch limo. Instead of Madonna or Hammer or someone else equally as exciting, they got. . .me.

We were escorted to the Turf Club and a table overlooking the finish line. Tom the smooth talker came by to introduce himself, and true to his word he had arranged for me to talk with The Man, Charlie Whittingham.

I had seen Charlie once in person some 20 years before. Jim was riding Quarter Horses at Los Alamitos at the time, and we took a day off to attend the races at Santa Anita as tourists. After parking our Volkswagen Beetle in the horsemen's parking lot, we walked past a trio of shiny black Rolls Royces lined up in a row. I was already impressed.

Heading for the entrance to the grandstand, we came face to face with Charlie Whittingham just as he exited the racing secretary's office. He was dressed in a suit and tie, his signature diamond stick pen twinkling mightily as it reflected back the rays of the afternoon sun. Nicknamed the Bald Eagle, Charlie and his uber-slick bald pate seemed just as majestic as our National Emblem, at least to my young eyes. He nodded a greeting, and I was star-struck. If I'd already had a racing program I would have asked for his autograph.

Over his entire career, Charlie started 13,796 horses whose combined earnings exceeded $109 million. He won the Kentucky Derby in 1986 with Ferdinand and in 1989 with Sunday Silence. This was horse racing royalty, and my memory of our brief sighting had him being at least six and a half feet tall and walking in a halo of light.

And now Charlie Whittingham was leaning on the railing surrounding our table in the Turf Club. I suddenly felt very

99

foolish. What was he going to think of me? Asking for advice from Charlie Whittingham! Nevertheless, he was friendly and took the time to put us at ease by relating what seemed like a series of tall tales, but with Charlie they were absolutely true stories.

That afternoon I learned Charlie's way of giving advice. He didn't teach by preach. Charlie told stories. If you listened, you would soon discover his advice embedded within the lines of these amazing stories he related so blithely.

Charlie made one thing very clear. In his opinion, time spent training over the Churchill surface was very valuable time, the more the better. When he told his Ferdinand story, he made no less than two references to the horse needing time to get used to the racing surface at Churchill Downs. He explained that Churchill Downs was different from almost every track he'd ever seen, and he had been on more than his fair share. Charlie related that Ferdinand had come back blowing hard and in obvious distress after galloping on the track for the first time. He made his opinion clear: A horse that was fit to run on another track wasn't necessarily fit to run on Churchill's track.

Charlie went on to say Churchill Downs was a good track, kind on the horses, and added the Kentucky rules of racing were particularly civilized, apparently referring to the similarity between California and Kentucky rules of racing.

As we exited the Turf Club, our limo was waiting, a perfect ending to a very unusual day at the races—a day that had found us the beneficiary of Charlie Whittingham's experience and wisdom.

It didn't take long for the powers that be at Golden Gate to hear about our day at Santa Anita. In fact the very next day, Sam Spear, the host of a local racing recap show, called to say he was representing Golden Gate Fields. Apparently, they were also interested in helping me make up my mind. In this case, they hoped I would continue to go forward with my original plan to run Casual Lies in the California Derby.

Unlike Santa Anita's position, they wanted me to realize that staying in Northern California with Casual Lies was in our best interest. To help me with my decision, would I like to spend a weekend in San Francisco? They would have a limo pick us up at our home and drive us the 35 miles to the city. In addition, they would arrange for us to stay at the Marriott at night and be their guests in the Golden Gate Fields Turf Club during the day. Oh, by the way, Ron McAnally would be there running one of his horses in the feature race, and it could be arranged for us to have a chat with him. Does any of this sound familiar?

Ron McAnally, who is still actively training as of this writing, has started over 17,626 horses with combined earnings totaling more than $123 million. He is best known as the trainer of the remarkable gelding John Henry. I thanked Sam for the invitation to the Turf Club and agreed we would enjoy having the opportunity to chat with Mr. McAnally. However, the limo and weekend really weren't necessary.

The Golden Gate officials involved in this offer must have had an interesting opinion of me as a trainer, particularly if they thought that a single afternoon of frivolity at either Santa Anita or Golden Gate could have swayed my decision in any way. They didn't need to try to outdo Santa Anita, and frankly I'm not sure they could.

I still don't know how Golden Gate found out about our day at Santa Anita. Frankly, while fun, it didn't really matter what either track offered in the way of enticements as they vied for my horse's participation—because ultimately the final decision would be based on what I felt was in the best interest of Casual Lies. That didn't mean I wasn't willing to listen when advice came from two such notable and experienced scions of racing as Charlie Whittingham and Ron McAnally.

So we spent a day in the Turf Club as the guests of Golden Gate Fields, I was delighted and honored when they asked me to present the trophy for the feature race. After we'd been shown to a private dining room with an unobstructed view of the racetrack, I looked up to see Jenny Craig headed our way. Accompanied by her husband, Sid, and a small entourage, they took the only other table on our level of a very private section of the Turf Club.

It was the first time I had seen her, other than on television when she used to do her own commercials. She was very petite and even prettier in person. She was wearing a classically cut black wool suit that matched her hair. The only other adornment she wore that I noticed was a stunning diamond brooch, about two inches square and gorgeously displayed against the black background. I told Jim you could bet it wasn't cubic zirconium.

As we were finishing lunch, the waiter came and asked if we would be interested in dessert. To this I responded, "Unless the chef could stuff celery stalks with cheesecake, I would have to pass." There was no way I was having a big gooey dessert with Jenny Craig sitting three feet from me. I did overhear her saying to one member of her party, "at least, eight glasses of water. . ." I didn't hear the rest. Maybe I could've had the cheesecake if I'd washed it down with eight glasses of water.

As promised, I did indeed get the opportunity to talk to Ron McAnally about his experiences in Kentucky. I'm sure when Bob Umphrey arranged this meeting, he probably didn't plan on Ron giving me virtually the same advice as Charlie—minus the entertaining stories.

It was clear that the racing surface in Kentucky was a huge issue as far as these two venerable giants of racing were concerned. Because of the time needed to acclimate to the Churchill surface, Ron and Charlie both felt that Santa Anita was the best place for my horse—that is, if we wanted to have a fighting chance at the Kentucky Derby.

The reasoning was quite simple—it was all about the timing. The Santa Anita Derby was on April 4, the California Derby would run on April 11, and the Kentucky Derby was always the first Saturday in May, taking place on May 2 in 1992.

Running at Santa Anita would give us another whole week to recover from the rigors of running in a really tough race. That was crucial when factoring in the need to ship more than two thousand miles and leave plenty of time for Stanley to become used to the Churchill surface.

Thus, I made a well-informed decision to run Casual Lies in the Santa Anita Derby. Next I needed to plan and carry out preparations for us to be away from home for an extended amount of time. If we ran well at Santa Anita and went on to Kentucky, we might not be coming back to Pleasanton for months. I would have to break up my stable and place my other horses, at least temporarily, with trainers I respected and trusted.

Shortly after I announced my intention to run Casual Lies in the Santa Anita Derby, I received a call from ABC Sports. They wanted to send a camera crew to Pleasanton to shoot some film for the upcoming Kentucky Derby. As I still hadn't decided on Kentucky, I wasn't overjoyed at the thought. They were persuasive, however, and showed up during training hours, something that didn't set too well with all the horsemen trying to get to the track. They wanted shots of Casual Lies outside of his stall with me on the lead shank. Stanley was ecstatic. Lots of stampeding around ensued until I finally called an end to the brouhaha before either one of us got hurt.

The morning we left for Santa Anita, Jim and I were up and at the barn even earlier than usual. Driving a pickup with a horse trailer and Stanley in tow, we wanted to avoid the Los Angeles commuter traffic when we got there later in the day, but people kept dropping by, delaying our departure, wishing us the best of luck while encouraging us to be sure to win one for the little people.

I wasn't prepared for what happened as we started driving down the road that divided the Pleasanton barn area—and I still shake my head in wonder and amazement at what occurred. On both sides of the road, standing at the ends of their barns, were the people of the backside. They waved and shouted, "Go get 'em, Shelley," "We love you, Stanley," and an abundance of good lucks. Somebody actually had a sign, hand drawn in a multitude of colors, which read: "Casual Lies Wins the Derby!"

It was like a parade. Smiling and waving back, I was truly overwhelmed as I drove my rig past the people we had worked alongside for so many years. We were going to find out soon enough that this joyous and wondrous sendoff, so filled with warmth and camaraderie, was going to have to last us for a while.

~

JIM AND I WERE EXCITED, hopeful and relieved when we pulled into the barn area at Santa Anita many hours later. Unfortunately we had not missed the commuter traffic as we had hoped and the tedious stop and go had added at least an hour to our already lengthy journey from Northern California. At one point in the heavy traffic we had narrowly missed a disaster when a car jerked over into the space I had left open in front of us. The driver then slammed on the brakes, and I wasn't going to be able to avoid colliding with him. Instinctively I glanced in my side mirror and jerked my rig into the next lane, where there was a glimmer of daylight. Fortunately for us, an astute driver in that lane was already slamming on his brakes, having perceived the possibility of a disastrous collision.

I could hear Stanley scrambling and thumping around in the back, and since there was nowhere to pull over, I could only hope he was still standing and uninjured. Jim turned around to look back through the window in the trailer and reported he could see Stanley peering back at him.

Shaken by our near miss, we continued on our way toward Santa Anita. Jim and I both knew how fragile life could be at times in racing—and here on a crowded freeway, the bad judgment of an impatient commuter could have caused serious injury to our fabulous horse in a moments passing. Approaching our destination, I noticed I still had a white-knuckled grip on the steering wheel.

As we settled in at Santa Anita Park in Arcadia, our new home at least for the time being, I was charmed by the ancient wooden barns with their dark green paint and white trim. Not surprisingly, we were the object of curiosity and considerable scrutiny from the moment we arrived.

One morning as I was mixing up a tub of grain, I spied Tom hustling through the barn area, emphasis on hustling. He seemed on a mission, since he looked neither left nor right as he headed toward his destination. I was certainly surprised to see him striding down the shedrow, straight toward me. I had just left his office two hours before, when

I'd hand-delivered Casual Lies' registration papers. Whatever could he want, I wondered.

Apparently Tom was receiving numerous reports about Shelley Riley and Casual Lies. One trainer in particular felt the need to tell Tom he thought Casual Lies was sore, if not lame. He had cornered Tom to express his doubts that my horse could make it through the Santa Anita Derby without breaking down.

I never found out for sure where this guy got his misinformation. Galvanized into action by this report, Tom had hustled right over to check it out for himself. The stories about the unknown, unheard of Northern California woman trainer of Casual Lies must have been ringing loudly in Tom's ears as he made his way to take a look for himself.

As we exchanged pleasantries in the shedrow, Stanley started up his bucking and squealing routine, mostly due to the delay in his grain tub making it to his stall. Tom got an eyeful of my big, bold colt, plainly on the muscle and the polar opposite of a horse too lame to run. Tom was visibly relieved as he told us why he had come by.

I was truly offended, but I had certainly learned one thing, that it wasn't going to be easy to make new friends at Santa Anita. Stanley, on the other hand, made a new friend on the very first day. A little golden-headed rooster made his way around the shedrow several times throughout the daylight hours. When he discovered Stanley's rice hulls, he must have thought he'd found a chicken's version of Shangri-La.

I didn't want this rooster in Stanley's stall for several reasons, not the least of which the diseases that chickens carry in their droppings. The other—and probably even more important issue—was that I didn't want Stanley getting attached to a companion animal that we would have to drag around with us everywhere we went. I tried running the rooster off, but he was always there when I returned to the barn. Although he still made his rounds of other barns, he frequently came back to sleep literally within inches of Stanley's back hooves as they both napped. Stanley never once tried to hurt him, and the rooster would wait under Stanley's feed tub, an opportunistic scavenger. Too bad for him—Stanley licked the tub, and there were never leftovers.

~

ON OUR FIRST MORNING AT Santa Anita I was on the lead shank walking Stanley while Jim cleaned his stall. At the far end of the barn, there was a tree filled with the noisiest bunch of scallywags I've ever heard. As it turned out, these were parrots that have thrived in the area for decades. This green feathered mob of hooligans would take off at the same time every morning, squawking and screeching. Flying above us with their rounded heads and stubby bodies, they looked remarkably like flying cigars. From day one, Stanley had more fun taking the opportunity to show off his wild side, anticipating the moment the yobbos took flight. Rearing up and striking, he tried to get his leg over the shank, bolting sideways and running backwards. I switched jobs with Jim in a big hurry. He could deal with the flying armada.

Charlie Whittingham came over to see Stanley right after we had arrived. After a few minutes of entertaining Stanley, Charlie invited us back to his barn to meet some of his protégés. We hung out with him as he fed hard peppermint candies to some of the best horses that ever stepped foot on a track. This wasn't why we had come to Santa Anita, but it was certainly a wonderful bonus in light of the unfortunate and sometimes unkind scrutiny we were going to be dealing with.

Women had a well-established presence in the stable area by this time, albeit there were very few female trainers or jockeys, percentage-wise. For a woman to have a horse of Stanley's quality was very unusual. Another oddity was a trainer going from no stakes horses to having a horse of this stature, a situation basically unheard of for either man or woman.

As time went by, I was increasingly astounded at how much controversy one horse and two people could stir up. The consensus of opinion was that we didn't belong. To this day I still don't completely understand it. Handicappers handicap, and that's their job, but some of their comments were so personal and unkind they were hurtful.

I was called inexperienced and a dreamer, while being described as someone running a mom-and-pop operation. It was inferred I was a hick, dumb and uppity—and those where the nicer comments. I received a call from one of my friends in Pleasanton who told me that a guy was running around the backside spouting, "That Shelley Riley, she thinks she so smart, and she's really nothing more than just another *womanist*." Okay. . .a womanist? I couldn't help myself—laughing until I hurt over that one.

Once their angst at our choosing the Santa Anita Derby over the California Derby began to fade, the Northern California public, and even the northern press to a certain extent, were embracing the underdog scenario. I began to get fan mail sent in care of the racing office or the stable gate. I cherished those missives from strangers who cared enough to take up pen and paper, writing their encouragement to Stanley and me. I still have all of them tucked away in a box of memories.

After the draw for Derby post positions, Santa Anita held a big press conference in front of the grandstand, at what they call Clockers' Corner. All the trainers were lined up at the head table with microphones so they could answer questions. I attended but sat in the crowd and didn't join in. I didn't want to be put in the position to defend my horse or myself once again, only this time in front of all my Southern California peers. It was just too painful.

On most days Jim and I spent a good portion of our time hiding out in our hotel, but it didn't help. The somewhat harsh and pithy observations about my horse and me only intensified as the race approached. Fair enough. I doubled up on the antacids every time I imagined how bad it could be in the saddling paddock, surrounded by Southern California racing fans, on race day.

Stanley kept eating, playing and looking forward to the flying cigars each day for his best opportunity to cut loose. His head, unlike mine, was totally in the right place, and as the big race day approached, it was obvious he was more than ready to run.

Chapter Eight
Fish or Cut Bait

Santa Anita does a remarkable job in promoting the Santa Anita Derby. Among other things in 1992, they ran full-page advertisements in the *Los Angeles Times* featuring caricatures depicting each horse entered in the race. When asked to interpret Casual Lies' more human characteristics for the caricature, I found it far easier than it might seem.

Casual Lies was a very kind horse who really liked people and, in particular, the attention they lavished on him. When the cameras came out, he was the first to strike a pose. The bigger the camera, the longer he seemed willing to cooperate. He would do anything for his adoring public—and was truly a shameless showoff.

In the caricature, lolling casually with his legs crossed, Casual Lies was seated at a bistro table with a glass of red wine. Resplendent in a beret and oversized sunglasses, he sported a carrot like a long cigarette holder and held at just the right angle. It was perfect. He looked like an Italian movie star with a self-satisfied smirk, one who was always preening just in case an adoring fan might be lurking nearby.

The Santa Anita marketing department produced large lapel buttons with these caricatures to distribute to the fans as they entered the grounds. They could pick their favorite pins and wear them during their day at the races. I still have one of the pins they handed out that day.

The scope of Derby day at Santa Anita far exceeded my expectations. Very nervous and ill at ease, I waited for Casual

110

Lies to arrive in the saddling paddock next to the jockeys' room. Once the saddling process is complete, the horses are led to a manicured walking ring, where they parade, their coats gleaming in the bright Southern California sunlight.

Well before the jockeys arrived in the walking ring, racing fans lined the fence on all sides to watch the stars on parade, both two-legged and four-legged. On this day, there were so many people crowded around the walking ring—more than 38,000 fans showed up for Santa Anita Derby day—that the noise and hubbub were actually alarming.

It was at this point my nerves really began to bite at my stomach. I was hoping we would be ignored again, but instinctively I knew this was not going to be the case. My dread grew with each step as I followed Jim and Stanley toward the overcrowded walking ring and into the brilliant rays of the afternoon sun.

Casual Lies had definitely shown up ready to run. He was on the muscle, coiled up like a panther and prepared to pounce. The sun shot copper sparks off his glistening coat as he pranced sideways around the walking ring. Neck arched, teeth grinding in anticipation, his muscles rippling—Casual Lies was nobody's pet. This was a warrior on his game and ready to do battle.

The center of the walking ring was congested with trainers, owners and their guests. While the horses circled, I was surrounded by chattering people, a celebratory group consisting of some of racing's elite—yet I stood alone. It felt like I was riding in the London Underground, crammed elbow to elbow with people I didn't know.

The sheer number of fans and their antics outside the walk ring was quite a show in itself. A few audacious individuals clamored up the light standards, clinging precariously to the slippery poles. When one particularly shrill voice caught my attention, I looked up to see a man straddling the fragile hooded lamp, high atop the slender pole. Unsteady on his perch, this daring man braced himself with one hand while waving mightily with the other, seemingly oblivious to the danger of injuring himself and the people below him if he fell. He alternated screaming my name with "Go get 'em, Stanley, show 'em what ya got!"

And he wasn't the only enthusiastic observer. I was surrounded by a vast landscape of smiling faces, and as I began to focus on individuals in the crowd, I realized just how many of those faces were involved in cheering for our team. Even though I was caught in a massive crowd of strangers, I began to comprehend that I wasn't isolated, and I certainly wasn't being ignored—quite the opposite in fact.

The fans were terrific, and I soaked up the goodwill like a flower overly long in the shade. Southern California racing fans were more than ready and certainly willing to cheer for the dark horse. As Jim led Casual Lies around the walking ring, I couldn't see them through the crowd, but I could keep track of their progress by the sound of the fans calling out my colt's nickname. Stanley had truly become the horse with two names.

~

WHEN I SAW A FEW OF THE jockeys squeezing through the crowd, I figured our jockey, Alan Patterson, wouldn't be far behind. But as I waited and waited, I began to get worried. Alan's business was riding in Northern California, and I had not seen him since I'd left Pleasanton. We had talked on the phone the previous day, and he advised he would be taking an early morning flight to Los Angeles after he worked some horses at Golden Gate Fields. Alan explained he wouldn't have time to stop in and see us at the barn, so he would go straight to the jocks' room when he arrived at Santa Anita.

When they called riders up and still no Alan, my feelings of alarm reached critical mass, and I started to push through the crowd looking for him. I was beginning to see the horses parading by with the jockeys already up and adjusting their stirrups, and still no Alan. Suddenly he appeared from out of the crush and brushed right past me. Hurrying after him, I tapped him on the shoulder to gain his attention.

I led him back to where Jim stood trying to control an increasingly agitated Casual Lies while I repeated the racing strategy he and I had discussed on the phone the night before. He quietly nodded his head as I gave him a leg up onto Stanley's back. Jim was leading them toward the racetrack when I saw Alan bend down and laugh at something Jim was saying. The air of excitement crushing down about us like a thick fog wasn't just agitating my horse—clearly it was affecting the whole team.

~

ONCE STANLEY WAS HANDED off to the ponygirl, he settled quickly to the task at hand, annoying the lead pony. While the horses warmed up, Jim and I made our way through the excited crowd to the clubhouse, and by the time we found our seats the field was already approaching the starting gate. My eyes were solely on my horse, willing him to behave as he was loaded into the gate. I saw him bullying the gateman just a tad, and though he broke well, he seemed just a little flatfooted. Bertrando shot out of the number one post and left there running, with Casual Lies right behind him in the seven-horse field.

Going into the first turn, Bertrando, who was co-favorite with A.P. Indy, still held the lead, and Casual Lies was laying third on the rail right behind him. Hickman Creek had moved up into second on the outside of us along with A.P. Indy, boxing us in. Just before the six-furlong pole, we were still third on the rail behind Bertrando with Hickman Creek running second on the outside of us. Although we remained in a box, there was a long way yet to go. A.P. Indy had been taken back off the fast early pace.

I saw Alan rise up in the stirrups and Stanley's head come up. Once Alan got Stanley back far enough to get to the outside, he let him accelerate again. A.P. Indy tried to go with us for a few strides, and then his rider, Eddie Delahoussaye, eased him back and angled him over to take the position we had vacated on the rail, a position that would enable him to save ground on the turn.

With Alan's continued encouragement, Casual Lies moved up strongly and ended up on the outside going around the turn. After saving ground, A.P. Indy moved to the outside of us down the lane, where he liked to run. He came abreast of Casual Lies and went head and head with us for a few strides before drawing away to win the race impressively by two lengths.

When it looked like we might close well enough to finish second, Bertrando hung on gamely and beat us by a very short neck.

My wonderfully brave horse followed the course chosen for him during the race and had laid it all out there that day giving everything he had. He finished third, beaten two lengths by A.P. Indy and that very short neck to Bertrando.

Bertrando had run with real determination, staying out of trouble on the front end of the race while saving ground hugging the rail. Our nemesis A.P. Indy looked impressive winning yet again. Casual Lies had showed up a lot of naysayers with a very courageous race against two seasoned, proven runners and possible favorites for the upcoming

Kentucky Derby.

Now what? two lengths is not a tremendous distance to make up, and racing luck can sure move a horse up two lengths or more in any race. We were very disappointed in not winning, but our question had been answered—sort of. Yes, we could run *with* the best. But could we outrun them? It was going to cost a lot of money to find out.

Casual Lies was still improving with each race, but we didn't want to go to Kentucky just to say we had run in the Kentucky Derby. We wanted to win! It would cost $10,000 to enter the Kentucky Derby and an additional $10,000 when the starting gate opened. Those were the set fees, and then we had to consider airfare for the horse and us, rental cars, hotels, licenses and many other expenses that add up when away from home. We simply didn't have unlimited means to chase an impossible dream.

I did feel that the money Casual Lies had earned should be used to secure his future, not just ours. The third-place finish in the Grade I Santa Anita Derby had added another $75,000, which brought Casual Lies' career earnings to a little over $400,000. A good finish in the Kentucky Derby would go a long way toward carving out a niche for him in Kentucky's stallion ranks. On the other hand, a dismal finish would erase a lot of the progress he had already made toward that goal. We were faced with a double-edged sword.

I discovered several things in our favor when I went to the test barn to watch Stanley cool out. I also had the opportunity to observe both A.P. Indy and Bertrando. I could see very clearly, at least in my opinion, neither of those horses had pulled up as well as we had. Stanley was tired, but he was alert and walked out very well with a sure stride and no sign of distress. He cooled out quickly, went through the testing process and was on his way in short order—the other two, not so much. They might not make the Derby at all from what I could see. It looked like A.P. Indy was stepping tenderly on the right front and Bertrando was having a great deal of trouble cooling out, which is usually not a good sign. All this was good information to have when it came time to make final decisions.

Back at our barn, we had mixed emotions about the day—relief that Stanley was safe and sound, and that he'd run a gutty race against terrific competition. But without a win I was still having reservations about the direction we should take going forward. Exhausted, I decided to sleep on the Kentucky decision. We still needed to consider the East coast horses that would be tough competition, not to mention Arazi in Europe.

The year before, Arazi had earned the Eclipse Award as the champion two-year-old male in the United States, as well as the Cartier award as two-year-old European champion colt. He was also named the Cartier Horse of the Year, the most prestigious award in European racing, an extremely rare honor for a two-year-old.

Although he had raced exclusively in France prior to the Breeders' Cup Juvenile, it was that race and the manner in which he won it that cemented his place as a superstar in the eyes of the world. Even with the rumors about his soundness after arthroscopic surgery to remove chips from both knees, Arazi could not be marginalized. After all, Arazi outran Bertrando in that Breeders' Cup Juvenile, opening up five lengths on the horse we had just finished behind in the Santa Anita Derby.

~

THE NEXT MORNING AT THEIR usual time, the resident band of green parrots lifted off, heading off to their next daily destination with a great deal of drama. Much-anticipated by Stanley, the squawking heathens provided the impetus for one of his robust and less than entertaining performances at the end of the shank. Once Stanley was safely back in his stall and the morning's chores were nearly done, I was raking the shedrow when I looked up and, to my utter amazement, saw Charlie Whittingham walking down my shedrow. I glanced behind me, and there wasn't anybody else around, so apparently he was looking for me. Metal rake in hand, I stood there transfixed by the sight of him.

"Well, what did you think?" he said without preamble as he stopped smack dab in the middle of the shredrow. "Have a little bad racing luck?"

"Uh, well, we didn't win," I replied.

"Ferdinand ran third in the Santa Anita Derby." He paused for dramatic effect. "Then there was The Derby." He was, of course, referring to Ferdinand's first-place finish in the 1986 Kentucky Derby.

"You think we ought to go?" I queried.

"I think you have to fish or cut bait," he said with that famous twinkle in his eyes. He then turned and walked away. I watched him disappear around the corner of the barn.

I must have looked like a Venus flytrap, standing there in the middle of the shedrow, mouth hanging open. I finally shut my mouth and looked at Jim, who had one eyebrow raised quizzically.

"Well, what do you suppose he meant by that?" I asked. "Do you think that was his way of telling us we ought to go?"

Jim shrugged and said, "Well, I guess that's as close as he's going to come."

Later in the day, as we were having lunch in the Turf Club, Charlie stopped by our box.

"Did you decide to fish or cut bait yet?" he asked.

"I don't know. What do you think?" I shot back.

He tipped his head toward his shoulder in a half shrug and went on his way. I wasn't going to get Charlie Whittingham to tell us, "Yes, you should run your horse in the Kentucky Derby." He already had in his own inimitable way. Truthfully I think Charlie enjoyed putting me off my game, what little I had.

No matter how optimistic my nature, I knew the opportunity to run a horse in the Kentucky Derby would most likely never come my way again. So in the end, I was unable to imagine sitting at home the first Saturday in May with my feet up as I watched the lost opportunity unfold on the television screen before me.

Who was I to deny that dreams really can come true? I stood in front of Stanley's stall and put my arms around his neck. As I rested my cheek against the warmth of his sleek muscles, I could feel his strength, vitality and the tremendous energy that just seemed to radiate out of every pore. Casual Lies had earned and, moreover, deserved my complete and total confidence. We were going to Kentucky, and we were going to run in the Kentucky Derby.

~

FINALLY, WHO WAS GOING TO ride Casual Lies in the Kentucky Derby? I left the decision up to Jim, just as he had left the decision to participate up to me. Jim had been the best jockey I had ever seen, and he had strong opinions about racing and the pressure racing can exert on a rider.

Jim talked to Chris McCarron, who said he was sorry, that he was already booked to ride for Ron McAnally. We were then encouraged to talk to Gary Stevens, whom we were told had been looking for a Derby mount. Gary had vast experience riding in the toughest venues around the world.

This included riding in and winning the 1988 Kentucky Derby with Winning Colors, a filly no less, along with a second-place finish in the 1991 Kentucky Derby aboard Best Pal. Jim admired Gary as a successful "big race rider" who had experience dealing with the often dangerous circumstances arising when as many as 20 horses are running on a narrow racetrack in front of more than 100,000 roaring fans.

Giving Alan the news that Gary Stevens would be riding Casual Lies was tremendously difficult. He was gracious and said he understood. Alan had picked the horse up out of the blue when Stanley's first jockey, Chance Rollins, had returned to Arizona and had benefited as I continued to name him on my horse, win or lose, through several more races. Jim had been taken off horses right after they had won, with no explanation. It is part of the game, just like owners changing trainers, but it is never an easy part.

Jim felt very strongly that Gary would give my horse the best chance at circumventing the treacherous conditions Stanley would surely face going into the most famous race for three-year-olds in the world.

The decision, once made public, was both popular and not so popular. Some people opined that I had finally made a good decision, a backhanded compliment to say the least. On the other hand, I received hate mail, not the first I had received. One person compared me to the Keating Five.

The vitriol that people can spew at those they don't even know, and without knowing the circumstances or the specifics, truly never fails to amaze me. It was around this time I remembered something attributed to Eleanor Roosevelt: "No one can make you feel inferior without your consent." The thought would be helpful again once I arrived in Louisville.

~

NEXT UP, HOW WE WERE going to get our horse to Kentucky? Transporting horses across country can be accomplished in only two ways—one is by van, the other by plane. Since we needed to get to Kentucky in the shortest possible time, with the least amount of wear and tear on Stanley, flying was our only real option.

By this time, I should have been buying antacid in 500-tablet bottles, what with stressing about stall bedding, jockeys, chickens, reporters, flying cigars and on and on. Putting my explosive horse on an airplane to soar above the clouds wasn't going to help. We had no idea what to expect.

Casual Lies was a perfect gentleman when shipping by van, so much so that he even refused to relieve himself while in transit. This had been a significant problem for us, since the travel time from stall to stall, Pleasanton to Los Angeles, had been about eight hours by horse trailer.

Stanley would be very anxious and restless by the time we arrived at our destination. Busting out of the trailer, he would drag whoever was on the lead shank to the nearest manure pile, where he spent several minutes. This doesn't sound like such a big deal, but actually it was. Stanley would be very quiet and out of sorts for about 24 hours after a long trailer ride.

Stanley was very fastidious, and frankly I think he didn't like splashing on himself in the trailer. I managed to cure this issue by bedding the trailer ankle deep in rice hulls and stopping at a rest stop halfway through the trip. I would hand-feed Stanley carrots through the door of the trailer until he relaxed enough to let go. When he had done it once, he was okay from then on. But now we faced a new mode of transport with very little idea of the time that would be involved.

I contracted with Tex Sutton Equine Air Service to fly Casual Lies to Kentucky. Stanley would be taken by van from Santa Anita to Ontario Airport and loaded onto a specially equipped DC-8 along with 16 other horses. They would touch down in Hot Springs, Arkansas, long enough to drop off and pick up a few horses. Once this exchange was completed, they would take off again and fly to Lexington, Kentucky. Another 16-horse van would be waiting at the airport in Lexington, where all the horses would be offloaded directly into the trailer without a single hoof touching down on the tarmac of either airfield. The horses would then continue the last leg of their trip, arriving at Churchill Downs about an hour later.

~

SINCE IT LOOKED LIKE WE might be gone for as long as three months, we decided that Jim would fly on to Kentucky with Stanley. I would drive the truck and trailer back to Pleasanton, tie up any loose ends and get everything organized so that we could feel comfortable being gone for that amount of time.

For several years, I raised a small number of pedigreed show cats, specifically British Shorthairs and Scottish Folds. MiMindsi Night Dreams, whom I called Odie, had been named Best British Shorthair both nationally and internationally, so it wasn't a case of being able to lock the doors and walk away for three months. Fortunately, my mother loved the cats as much as I did, and she did a great job with them. She put her own life on hold for those three months, taking care of business at home so we could chase after our dream. Without Mom, I would have had a much longer list of items to worry about.

The van was scheduled to pick Stanley and Jim up at 2 a.m. in the darkened Santa Anita barn area, and the flight was to leave at 5 a.m. Creeping around the barn area at 1 a.m. felt very strange. There's a peace and comfort about a backstretch at rest. The blending of all the smells—the horses, hay and even the manure pile—fill the night with quiet warmth. Whispering to one another we tried not to disturb anyone as we moved the tack trunk, equipment and feed out to the road to help speed up the process once the big rig arrived. Despite our attempts to maintain the peace, a few of the horses rustled around in their stalls. We could hear a few soft nickers of inquiry from various barns as the diesel rig with its throaty growl wound through the barn area toward us.

In short order the equipment was loaded, followed by Casual Lies, his first ride on an eighteen-wheeler. He walked up the steep ramp and backed into a stall like he had done it many times before. This was just the first of several new experiences he would face before the night was over.

I followed them out to the freeway with my disgruntled cat Odie, who had accompanied us to Santa Anita, in his crate on the jump seat of the pickup. This hour of the day was not civilized as far as he was concerned. Silky black with huge golden-flecked orange eyes, Odie was 16 pounds of muscled stud cat, and he had a thoroughly British penchant for showing his disdain when the occasion arose. Shown all over the United States and parts of Canada, he was not unfamiliar with traveling, but it didn't mean he appreciated being roused out of bed and stuffed into a cold travel crate in the middle of the night.

At the point where Jim and I would go our separate ways, I pulled over and watched as the van's lights faded into the distance. Although Jim was an amazing and talented horseman, he didn't do well attending to details, which was my forte. This would be the first time since we had started training Stanley that I wouldn't be in control, and as I sat in my idling pickup, I couldn't shake the feeling that something wasn't right about being separated from my horse.

~

WHEN I ARRIVED IN PLEASANTON, I found the Alameda County Fair Association board of directors, along with the manager of the Alameda County Fair, had arranged a sendoff cocktail party, with me as the guest of honor. I met several members of the board, who were tickled that Casual Lies training had begun at their facility.

The majority of our friends from the Pleasanton barn area attended the party. What was truly remarkable was the extent of their excitement and goodwill. A backside employee who called himself Red Jeep asked for my autograph. He had bright red hair, so I understood that part of the nickname. As to the rest, I can only guess, but he was certainly excited, maybe even more than I about all the events surrounding me and my horse.

The fair association had hung two huge white canvas banners with red lettering at the party. One said GOOD LUCK IN LOUISVILLE and the other THE HOME OF CASUAL LIES.

After the party, the banners would make their way to the stable gate, hung there for everyone to see as they entered the barn area. THE HOME OF CASUAL LIES banner went on to hang there for many years after.

~

WHILE I WENT HOME TO A CELEBRATION, Jim had to contend with

one snafu after another en route to Kentucky. He started with being forced to wait in the van on the tarmac at the airport for over an hour and a half before the van was allowed to approach the plane. A rising Z-shaped ramp was pulled up and was designed, at either end, to match the van and plane openings. Each horse had to step out of the van with his handler onto an elevated platform, then angle to the right and walk up a ramp to another platform. At this juncture, they turned left to cross a bridge and finally enter the plane.

Jim later told me that it was really scary crossing the bridge, with the side rails little more than chest high. If a horse were to pitch a fit, it was a long way down. Meanwhile, the sight and sounds of the planes taking off a short distance away contributed to the alien and frightening environment for these pampered and explosive racehorses.

The takeoff was rather abrupt, and while the horses tended to scramble a little, they were surprisingly good about it. Jim was ill prepared for how cold it was after they reached their cruising altitude, but on a horse flight, you can't complain to a flight attendant. It was, however, a breakfast flight, with cold drinks and self-serve sandwiches in a picnic cooler located behind the cockpit.

They hit some pretty heavy turbulence going into Hot Springs, with drops and bumps, but again the horses took it in stride. We had arranged for Stanley to have a stall and half, since he was such a big horse, so he was up at the front of the plane by himself. The rest of the plane was divided into stalls with narrow walkways down both sides of the plane and between each row of stalls for the grooms to stand and control their horses. All the flooring underfoot was covered with heavy-gauge rubber matting. The plane was full, and most of the grooms sacked out for some sleep. Jim, however, stayed in close contact with Stanley, keeping his hands on the lead shank, particularly when the flight got rough.

When they finally got to Churchill that afternoon, Stanley was very glad to see a stall at last. Jim, on the other hand, was completely taken aback by the bedding. Wood shavings! We had never bedded on shavings and had specifically asked for rice hulls.

It was the only stall bedded, and Jim had no choice. So in went a very tired Casual Lies. We would find out much later what a mistake this was. We had just hit the first obstacle on the yellow brick road, and what an obstacle it turned out to be.

Three days later, I carried all the warmth of the fairgrounds sendoff with me as I boarded the plane to Louisville, filled with hope and anxious to see Jim and my horse again. But I still had a nagging feeling that I had needed to be there, that I should have been waiting for them when they arrived.

The clock was ticking toward midnight, and the fancy dress ball was rushing to a conclusion. I wasn't to know how badly cracked the glass slipper was as I flew into the night.

Chapter Nine

Kentucky

Apparently the long trip to Kentucky hadn't slowed Stanley down for long—he was feeling terrific. According to Jim, he had pulled up from the Santa Anita Derby and the airplane trip like they had been gambols in the park. Snorting and blowing, he would stampede to the end of the shank at the slightest provocation. No matter what we had in mind, Stanley didn't seem to think he needed to rest.

While I was staying busy in Pleasanton, Jim and Stanley settled into their new environment in Louisville, and Jim was calling with updates on a daily basis. He said it was fortunate we had packed a stall fan along with our other equipment because it was extremely hot and humid. Having been raised in Lone Pine, California, which is high desert country, Jim knew a thing or two about hot weather.

Jim voiced his concern over the wood shavings in Stanley's stall, that they were extremely dusty and had a distinct chemical smell that Jim found unsettling. Because making sudden changes in a horse's feed is never a good idea, we had loaded enough hay and grain on the plane to get us by, but the lack of room for the bulky rice hulls had made it necessary to rely upon Churchill Downs for Stanley's special bedding. Unfortunately, the track hadn't been able to accommodate our request and had substituted the wood shavings. Jim asked the feed man every morning about the rice hulls, and every morning the guy said he would keep trying—but he wasn't having much luck.

When I finally arrived in Louisville a full three days after Casual Lies and Jim, it was the middle of the night, and a sharp, cold wind bit at my skin. I was ill prepared for the chilly weather.

No matter the lateness of the hour, I went straight to the track from the airport. I needed to see Casual Lies with my own eyes and get a feel for how he was doing. As I walked up to his stall, Stanley was snuffling around in the shavings. When I called his name, his head came up and he rushed over to get a hug and a rub behind his ears and under his throat. Of course, right off the bat he tried to get my fingers in his mouth. Those rubbery lips of his were always as busy as a chimpanzee's.

When I hugged him around the neck, he hooked his head over my shoulder so he could keep me close for as long as he possibly could. Being tucked under his jaw kept me from being nipped, but at the same time, it gave him the perfect angle for grabbing part of my clothing, which he did.

After I pried my sleeve from Stanley's teeth, I put a lightweight blanket on him to wear for the remainder of the night in case the weather turned even colder. It wasn't a warm night sheet, but it had to do because it was the only one we had brought with us. After I closed up the bottom door on his stall and headed out, Stanley nickered and banged his hoof against the door to protest my departure.

Just a few hours later, when Jim and I arrived at the barn around 4:30 a.m., the wind had picked up and was blowing directly into Stanley's stall. He resembled a huge beaver with his short California coat stuck straight up, it was obvious the lightweight sheet was failing to keep Stanley warm—he was miserable.

When Jim had topped off Stanley's water the night

before, he said it was so hot he had seriously considered leaving the stall fan on for the night—but then the night had turned cold. Such is Kentucky weather in the spring. If you don't like it, wait 15 minutes because it is certain to change.

When the tack shop opened, we were its first customers. We bought a quilted horse blanket to replace the light sheet we had brought with us from California. The blanket was an expensive equine version of an Alpine ski jacket, but the price was no object, of course. Stanley was soon toasty warm and munching contentedly in his stall. Having attended to our number one priority, the care of my horse, Jim and I headed off to the track.

The first time I saw the track at Churchill Downs, I was aghast. The dirt was the color of a manila envelope and looked deep and tiring. It seemed apparent immediately that this was a surface you definitely needed to train on before you ran on it. No doubt about it, Charlie Whittingham and Ron McAnally had both given me very sound advice regarding this racetrack.

When we galloped Stanley the first time, Jim kept him under a firm hold while I anxiously followed their progress from where I stood by the clocker stand on the outside rail near the half-mile pole.

When they came off the track, Stanley did seem to be blowing more than I thought he should, certainly for his level of fitness. However, he adjusted to the new surface fairly quickly, and we found that the racetrack's looks were deceiving. Churchill Down's racetrack is actually a very kind track on a horse, once he's fit.

Stanley's first work over the surface wasn't very impressive, time wise, but then he never had been much of a workhorse when he didn't have company to put him on his toes. I did, however, feel this surface would suit a powerful horse like Casual Lies because instead of skimming across the surface, he attacked it and pulled it to him with an easy grace. Churchill's surface really reminded me of a deeper version of Golden Gate Fields, and Stanley loved Golden Gate Fields. As I watched my horse train over the surface, I was feeling very confident and more assured that I had made the right choice in coming to Kentucky.

~

IT WAS STILL TOO EARLY IN the Kentucky Derby season for significant numbers of reporters or crowds of people. The big influx would start showing up about two weeks before the Derby. So we toured the breeding farms and caught up on our favorite novels, which we never seemed to have time to read. It was a nice respite from the hustle and bustle we had experienced at Santa Anita, and the whole team, all three of us, needed this quiet time.

Eventually a few reporters started to trickle in. One of the first was Steve Haskin from the *Daily Racing Form*. I had talked with him on the phone a few times about Casual Lies, but mostly I had talked to another Steve from the *Form*, Steve Feldman. Steve and Steve were writing a weekly column called the *Derby Watch*.

They tracked the progress of the horses that were most likely to end up in Kentucky the first Saturday in May. Steve Haskin showed up at our barn one morning and asked me if I would be interested in writing a diary leading up to the Kentucky Derby, a daily journal that would be published in the *Daily Racing Form*. I could write whatever I pleased, although space was limited and I would have to be brief. I wasn't overly enthusiastic at first, in part due to the drubbing I had taken at the hands of various publications in Southern California.

I didn't warm up to Steve right off. I don't know why exactly—maybe because he represented the press and I didn't particularly trust them anymore. They could and would feed off you with an unholy glee. But I bless Steve's persistence. I can say without reservation that Steve Haskin is one of only a handful of people we met during our Kentucky adventure whom I came to consider a true friend, not just a casual acquaintance.

It's because of Steve Haskin that I decided to open up to the press and share our experiences for the benefit of the racing public. If I hadn't, I can truthfully say I would have missed the time of my life cowering in my tack room trying to avoid the media.

Steve's persistence eventually convinced me that a diary was an opportunity to show the non-racing public a side of the sport that they didn't often get to see. He told me it would help racing all over the country. Thus, I began writing down my thoughts and experiences as we went along. I took the job very seriously and tried very hard to be a happy and joyous voice for racing.

Shortly after arriving at the barn one morning, while I was walking Stanley around the shedrow, I was greeted with a broad smile and a cheery salutation from Neil Drysdale, the trainer of A.P. Indy. Hmmm, I had read he was an ogre with a perpetual frown and an unpredictable temper. Needless to say, after that portrayal by the press, I was a little taken aback when I first found out Neil Drysdale and I would be sharing the same barn at Churchill Downs.

Being stabled next to someone and sharing the shedrow is like being neighbors in a duplex. You very quickly learn everything you didn't want to know about all of your neighbor's habits. Like a good marriage, one neighbor usually gives more to make it an equal partnership and thus ensure the peace is kept. I can't say Neil was the best neighbor I've ever had, but he was equally as good. We walked hots together, raked the shedrow together and even picked up rocks together. I discovered he spoke flawless Spanish, with an Argentinean accent. I speak it with an O accent—put-o the horse-o in the stall-o.

On that first meeting, he graciously offered me any help that I might need while he took a thorough survey of my horse. As time went by, he even gave me some tips on the press. I wasn't sure I was totally ready for the Neil Drysdale school on press relations. He confessed, with a smile, that he'd read the press had found his personality as cold as a frosty Mint Julep. As I watched him with the reporters who came by his barn on a daily basis, visions of a hot toddy didn't come to mind, but I witnessed style, dignity and most certainly a very pleasant demeanor.

~

THE DERBY BARNS, WHERE all the eligible Kentucky Derby horses were stabled at that time, were located near the end of the vast barn area, far away from the constant traffic found around the main stable gate entrance. Bordering our barn was a fairly large grassy area, where it was possible to take a few horses out at a time, letting them enjoy the sun, graze lightly and just relax. The area sported a few trees, and even though a public road paralleled the other side of the fence, it was very peaceful. It became a daily ritual for Stanley to graze in the sun for 20 minutes or so, mostly in the afternoon.

As Jim and I began to settle into our temporary life at Churchill Downs, it quickly became apparent that Casual Lies was changing, and not for the better. He was getting very quiet, which was not like him. When we first began taking him out onto the grassy area, it was hard to get him to stop playing long enough to graze. But as the days went by he began to show very little interest in the things that used to make him crazy.

My intuition antenna perked up. I had begun to pick up the beginnings of distress signals, but I couldn't put a finger on where they were originating. It was certainly puzzling. Casual Lies still looked great. He was galloping well, and his legs were cold—but such a big change in his personality couldn't be ignored.

The last piece of the puzzle would fall into place, and provide the answer I was seeking, when we worked Casual Lies in company with another horse. When we needed a horse to work with Stanley, Julien "Buck" Wheat kindly arranged it for us.

In fact whenever we needed anything at all, Buck Wheat was there to help. Known as the "Mayor of the Backside," Buck worked as Churchill Downs' director of horsemen's relations for more than 60 years until his death in 2011 and was an all-around great guy. He was there at a drop of a hat in his golf cart to smooth the way, no matter the need. He befriended Jim, Stanley and me the first time he stepped out of his cart at our barn.

Not everybody is eager to work their horse with a Kentucky Derby hopeful, but when Buck spoke with Murray Johnson, a local trainer with some good horses, Murray agreed and Buck set it up for us. The morning of the workout, we agreed we would give the other horse a five-length head start so that both horses would get something out of their work.

The pair of horses backtracked together in their warm-up. They then turned and galloped around to the seven-eighths pole, where they would break off as arranged. All went well at first. They got off in good order, with the other horse five body lengths ahead of us. But to our great dismay, Casual Lies never caught his company in the workout, and his company was a maiden.

Stanley's dismal workout was the talk of the backstretch, but we couldn't have cared less what was being said. Our suspicions were confirmed—we were sure we were in trouble now. Stanley was obviously distressed when he got back to the barn. His legs looked great, and he wasn't coughing, which would have indicated the possibility of the pulmonary bleeding known as exercised-induced pulmonary hemorrhage (EIPH), more commonly referred to around the track as bleeding. But this was definitely not what was bothering him.

Jim said Stanley felt fine, soundness-wise, during the workout. He just wouldn't pick up the bit, and he never tried to work. By the time we bathed him, cooled him out and returned him to his stall, he was, if anything, worse. As we hovered by his stall, Stanley munched at his favorite alfalfa quietly, without his usual alacrity. Then he quit altogether and just stood in the middle of the stall with his head down. When we started hearing his stomach all the way out in the shedrow, we called in Dr. Gary Lavin, a local veterinarian.

Dr. Lavin was flabbergasted, pointing out he wasn't going to need his stethoscope to hear Stanley's stomach gurgling and popping. As he stood next to us in the shedrow, he likened Stanley's stomach noise to the sounds of a Maytag washing machine. Nevertheless, he did a thorough exam with his stethoscope, shaking his head as he went along. He would ask a question every so often and I would answer.

"No, he doesn't have a temperature."

"No, he doesn't have diarrhea."

"No, there was no change in his diet. We still have feed

left that we brought with us from California."

Then I looked down and pointed, "The only thing that is different is the bedding. I suppose he could be eating some of the wood shavings when he is scrounging around looking for scraps from his feed."

Dr. Lavin took blood for analysis and gave Stanley some medication for the obvious pain in his stomach. He was trying to ward off a more serious colic than Stanley already had. We all agreed that, barring any other symptoms, he had probably had an allergic reaction to the chemicals in the shavings. Dr. Lavin came back every two hours to check on Stanley until we were sure that things weren't getting worse.

Since we still couldn't get rice hulls, we stripped the stall of the wood shavings and bedded him on timothy hay. Timothy per bale is very expensive at the racetrack, but it is high in fiber and doesn't put the weight on like other feeds. I had changed Stanley's bedding from straw to timothy prior to the Hollywood Futurity in Southern California. At that time he was chowing down straw like it was horse candy, which had definitely kept him too chunky. I hoped the timothy would help him once again.

We had less than two weeks before the Kentucky Derby. Was our dream dead? If the toxins left Stanley's system quickly, his stomach would settle down and he should be fine. Still, we could lose a considerable amount of training time. I had to ask myself, would Stanley be able to lose important training time, overcome a very serious allergic reaction and still be able to run in the toughest three-year-old race in the world?

Jim thought not. He was ready to pack up and go home. I remained calm on the surface for Jim's sake, but I was doubtful myself. Since we were already there, I told Jim I could see no reason why we shouldn't stay and see what happened. If we didn't run, then it wasn't meant to be. We could watch the big race from the barn area. However, if we left and he started bucking and kicking two days after we returned to California, we would feel very foolish. Jim was adamant. He wanted to get out of town, and he felt that there was no way Stanley could run without training. So I pulled out the big gun and pointed out that it wouldn't be wise to move Stanley just yet—he was stressed enough.

With the removal of the wood shavings, Dr. Lavin's expertise and Stanley's fantastic metabolism, my colt recovered quickly. We had made it through the forest, we'd survived the field of poppies, and the Emerald City was in sight. There was no getting around the fact that we had lost a week of training and that the next few days were going to be crucial. On another front, I was still fighting Jim's desire to go straight back to California.

~

DURING THE WEEK THERE was very little for us to do around the barn other than monitor Stanley for signs of improvement. Jim and I were amused to watch reporters prowl around looking for some juicy bits of news. Not unlike a piece of carrion in the hot sun on the desert floor, a trainer pausing long enough to be interviewed was soon surrounded.

While we weren't completely ignored in the beginning, they soon found out that a maiden had outworked Casual Lies and that I was claiming he had an allergic reaction. So every time he was out of the stall, he was an object of interest. Since the reporters certainly didn't think we had a shot to win the Derby, I could only guess that they must have been angling for some kind of story cut from our current unfortunate circumstances.

The days passed, and a trickle of reporters became a flood

as the world's press began to pour in to join the ranks of the U.S. media already on site. Arazi's arrival from Europe was imminent.

The number of reporters who found their way to our barn began to increase as their numbers in the barn area began to swell overall. With the advice and encouragement I'd received from the *Daily Racing Form's* Steve Haskin, I was happy enough to talk to them, at least at first.

As they waited with pens in hand, firing off questions that weren't always designed to be flattering, I recalled how I had been called stupid, crazy and even a liar. It had been reported I had stars in my eyes and unrealistic expectations. It was at that point I made the decision to change my approach—I decided to see the funny side of their questions. Witty repartee would be my best defense as well as offense. I was going to unveil my hidden inner comedienne.

Soon, to my amazement, and perhaps due to my change in attitude, reporters not only surrounded me—they were standing three deep.

Fortunately barricades had been added to all the barns, a welcome addition to the 24-hour security guards who had arrived to keep our horses safe when we couldn't be there. All who approached the barns, media included, were advised they must stay behind the barricades to ensure at least a semblance of normalcy for the horses.

But there is nothing normal about dozens of people coming to stand behind the barricades each day, and only a few feet separating them from my horse's stall. Although there was constant commotion, Churchill Downs officials did everything they could to help all of us cope. Still, the press must be able to get their stories, and we as trainers must cooperate for the sake of the fans. The Kentucky Derby is good for the sport, and the media are the spokesmen to our fans. Whereas I was a reluctant but willing participant in all this, there was nothing reluctant about Stanley's involvement.

Casual Lies loved people, and he loved it when people came by to visit. So Kentucky was a source of constant entertainment for him. He never tired of watching the people—the more the better. He was such a poser—the snap of a shutter was sure to stop him in his tracks. He was definitely an ambassador of the sport in his own right.

~

THE DAY FINALLY CAME WHEN the arrival of Arazi was upon us, and every possible form of news media was beating itself into a frenzy. It seemed as though a comet were about to hit Louisville. It was announced when his plane took off from Paris and when it was scheduled to arrive. We were assured that there would be live coverage of the landing, deplaning and subsequent arrival at the Churchill Downs detention barn, where horses flown in from other countries were quarantined for a period of time.

Arazi was the main topic of conversation at the racetrack. Most of the horsemen were inclined to be a little more reserved than the media. We were all excited to see last year's star, but the majority weren't prepared to accept that Arazi was the second coming of Secretariat. He had been gone a long time, and his races in Europe were hard to figure. The overall consensus of the horsemen was: "Let's see him run one more time before we fall on our knees."

And so Arazi arrived to much fanfare. I was asked why I thought there was such a widespread conviction on the part of the public that Arazi was unbeatable. I opined, for what it was worth, in my opinion the public wanted a star.

Arazi had all the ingredients to be a very bright media

star. It certainly didn't hurt to have the mystique of training in a romantic forest in France. His connections were everything that Casual Lies' weren't. His breeder was the owner of the NFL Buffalo Bills, Ralph C. Wilson, who sold him as a weanling for $350,000 to Allen E. Paulson, the chairman of Gulfstream Aerospace. Paulson named the colt after an aeronautical navigation checkpoint in the Arizona desert and accepted an offer of $9 million from Sheikh Mohammed Bin Rashid Al Maktoum for a half interest in Arazi even before the colt had won the 1991 Breeders' Cup Juvenile, theoretically valuing Arazi at $18 million prior to that win.

I was also asked if I really thought my horse could outrun Arazi. It would have been too easy to say even Secretariat got beat or that a lot of things can go wrong in a 20-horse field. I could've said he hadn't run fast enough in Europe and that he wouldn't be fit, even with trainer Francois Boutin's expert efforts at conditioning him. It certainly wasn't a secret he'd had knee surgery and that he was not physically correct by any means. There was the possibility that he might be unsound yet again. For the most part, however, I tried to keep those opinions to myself.

I certainly had to think about one particular horse that Arazi had beaten in the Breeders' Cup the year before—that horse was Bertrando. He'd shown us he didn't know how to quit in the Santa Anita Derby, and yet Arazi had jerked his head off in the Breeders' Cup Juvenile.

As I watched the really big show unfolding about me, I couldn't help contemplating the once-in-a-lifetime opportunity of training a horse of Casual Lies caliber. I thought about that because, as a small operator and a woman to boot, in all likelihood I was living through my first and only chance to run in this historic race. Even Charlie

Whittingham said Kentucky Derby horses didn't come along all that often. If that was true for Charlie Whittingham, where did that leave me?

Training horses means working seven days a week, 365 days a year. Another trainer and close friend once said, "You can't let the horses take over your life." The reality was that not only had training taken over my entire life, Casual Lies had become the very center of my existence.

If Casual Lies was the lightning in the bottle, my greatest fear was the possibility of the bottle cracking, the lightning escaping and the chance of his Derby appearance passing me by. His close brush with colic had been a reminder, once again, of just how fragile the bottle was.

As the allergic reaction had proved, Casual Lies was no more a machine than A.P. Indy, Arazi or any other Kentucky Derby hopeful. The decisions Neil Drysdale, Francois Boutin or any of us made could not guarantee Derby success. No matter how much the best one horse may appear to be, luck and circumstance play far too great a role in the outcome of this great race and was one of the biggest reasons why winning the race was coveted by so many.

I kept my focus on saving Stanley's one chance—our one chance—at taking part in this historic event. Of course, if I had let all the so-called experts make my decisions for me, I would never have run Casual Lies anywhere but on the county fairs. I couldn't let the head games affect my decisions now. The handicappers I'd heard and comments I'd read, including one made by another trainer of a Derby horse, kept repeating, "If the French horse came, the rest of the horses may as well stay in their stalls." Patrick Valenzuela, Arazi's jockey, was quoted as saying, "Every other horse in the race is running for second."

As I sat there thinking my thoughts and watching my

horse come back to life, despite what the experts thought our chances were, I was still hoping we could stay on track and Stanley would be well enough to train and run to win like I knew he could. My biggest hope was that luck would be smiling on us that first Saturday in May and we would actually get our one chance at the Run for the Roses.

Chapter Ten

What a Buildup

Stanley was back in the saddle, so to speak, on his toes and eager to please. He was training forwardly once again, and I couldn't have been more thankful, on so many levels. Obviously Stanley meant more to me than any single race ever would. To see him bright-eyed as ever while displaying his special brand of joy at just being alive was reward in itself. Our dream wasn't dead yet, not by any means. Thanks to my colt's recuperative abilities, our dream was very much alive.

Once I had turned off the shy side and turned on the funny side of Shelley, the word had spread like wildfire that my barn was a great place to get a good quote and that I could be entertaining and loquacious. Subsequently, my end of the barn was turning into a hangout for all the celebrities, since virtually every reporter on the grounds showed up at least once each morning. The dignitaries had also arrived by now, and they were out mingling with celebrities and the press. The backside began to take on the air of a film festival—people seeing and being seen. I watched the parade every chance I got, which wasn't often, until I was asked to join in again, which was most of the time.

I was called up to the racing office one morning and given a message to phone the producers of ABC television's popular *The Home Show*, starring Gary Collins and Sarah Purcell. Much to my amazement when I returned their call, they informed me I had been selected to be the Woman of

Distinction for the show that would be broadcasting live from Churchill Downs. What they had in mind was a short video piece used as an introduction, with insight about Shelley Riley as she prepared to run her horse in the Kentucky Derby. In addition, after airing the taped segment, Gary would be interviewing me live on the day of the broadcast. I could expect the television crew's arrival at my barn by the end of the week. The crew would spend several days with us.

When I got back to the barn and told Jim the story, I mentioned that the interviewer with the television crew would be an ex-football player. He asked who it was.

"Uh, I think it was Larry Swann," I said, not quite remembering everything they had told me.

"Who?"

"Larry Swann," I repeated with a shrug.

"Do you mean Lynn Swann?" Jim asked, his eyes widening.

"Yeah, I guess so," I replied with another shrug.

The quintessential football fan, Jim became very excited. He couldn't believe I didn't know Lynn Swann, and he was over the moon that we were going to meet the former NFL wide receiver who'd won four Super Bowl rings.

If I didn't know who Lynn Swann was then, I certainly knew by the end of the week. The day he first walked up to the barn, without being introduced, I could tell who he was— he had so much star quality about him. We hadn't known what to expect, and what we got was an extremely friendly, outgoing and down-to-earth guy. It took us about 32 seconds to build a rapport, and away we went on a trip through the amazingly engaging Lynn Swann house of fun.

Lynn could pull the sun out from behind a cloud with his sheer presence alone. The three of us acted silly, and we didn't care who thought so. It was a nice time away from the pressure cooker in which we were living, and we behaved like a bunch of college freshmen on our first spring break—well, without the booze and beach volleyball, that is.

We had a camera crew with us everywhere we went, but Lynn was so comfortable to be around that we didn't worry, nor did we even pay them that much attention. It was their job to keep up with us, and we certainly did keep them hopping. I could only hope we could trust them to edit us whenever we got too outrageous.

Lynn came out one morning while I was in the middle of cleaning Stanley's stall, and he jumped in, intent on helping me. A 15-minute job ended up taking two hours, with considerable clowning around and gales of laughter. We didn't do a very good job either. We did, however, entertain a whole lot of people as we carted the muck basket filled to overflowing with soiled bedding to the manure pile. The audience included LeRoy Jolley, Charlsie Cantey and Allen Jerkens, who were all hanging around my barn at the time. They decided Lynn had missed his true calling as a stall mucker.

At one point, twenty or more reporters were standing behind the barricade at my barn while I stood in the shedrow in front of Stanley's stall. They were firing questions at me, and I was fielding them, enjoying myself as I included the occasional wisecrack or two while trying to keep things as lighthearted as possible. Someone walked up and said Arazi would be on his way to the track in 15 minutes. As one, Jim, Lynn, camera crew and I dropped everything and hustled off to watch, right along with everyone else. It was like flotsam bearing down on the shore as we rushed toward the track.

We all walked in sync, headed in the same direction, and joined several hundred people who were also intent on seeing Arazi set his first golden hoof onto the track.

As we moved along, I heard one reporter walking behind us comment to another, "Man, I got more from her in 15 minutes than I got from all the other trainers combined in the last three hours." I glanced back at the speaker and realized he was one of the many faces I had just been entertaining across the barricade at my barn. They were talking about me, and frankly I wasn't totally sure that was a good thing.

Once we reached the track, we couldn't find any place open on the rail. Lucky for us, we had Lynn Swann and camera crew with us. Lynn just squeezed into a small opening at the rail, and when he did, people began making room for us as though he had parted the sea. I could see why he was so good in the NFL.

We couldn't hear Arazi making his way to the track, although we heard the sound of feet running and scuffling on the gravel surface as news cameramen scampered around for their shots of the famous colt. The majority of people along the rail were leaning in the direction of the sounds made by the cameramen, craning their necks and straining to get a look at the legend. Buying into the excitement, my expectations were such that I was almost disappointed there wasn't a herald with a banner-draped horn announcing the cavalcade of Arazi and his media entourage when they finally surged into view.

Ridden by his groom and led by another stable lad, Arazi turned out to be a slight and rather nondescript colt, chestnut in color with a white blaze on his pretty face. Decked out with red bandages on his legs, he sported a blue blanket over his flanks in the European style. Frankly, I wasn't as impressed with the looks of the horse as I was with the media blitzkrieg dogging his heels.

The colt seemed to handle the mob well enough at first. Then he stepped onto the track and proceeded to display some very bad manners, wheeling and sucking back so deeply and hard that he almost went down. I'd heard he had done this when he was at Churchill Downs for the Breeders' Cup and had succeeded in unloading his rider, Patrick Valenzuela, prior to a workout. History was to repeat itself when, a few days later, Valenzuela was aboard for a scheduled workout—at least for a while—and Arazi pulled that nasty little trick once again, dumping the rider.

The press was delighted. As far as they were concerned, this was just another omen that Arazi was totally on his game. Thus, his winning the Kentucky Derby was pretty much a foregone conclusion, while the rest of us were there to serve as also-rans.   ~

As the days went by, Arazi began to unravel. It became obvious he was not handling the long trip, the new home and the mass of unending attention. He began to shrink more and more each time we saw him. Never a large horse—in fact, a small horse by anyone's standards—he became downright peaked. I felt very sure that this little guy could never get by my 1,100-pound horse.

The media, however, ignored all the signs and the rumors that were going around. They had built this horse up so much that they couldn't back down now.

For example, Andy Beyer, Casual Lies' most ardent detractor, wrote: "Casual Lies is simply not good enough to win the Kentucky Derby." But then he also said all the California horses should have stayed in California, which, of course, included A.P. Indy and Bertrando. Beyer felt that Arazi was going to win by so far it would look like Secretariat's Belmont Stakes.

It was time to test the pudding. Casual Lies had been galloping like a dynamo, and I had scheduled him to work five-eighths of a mile with company. If Stanley worked well and cooled out satisfactorily, we would know he was 100% and back to himself.

We decided to put Gary Stevens up on Stanley for the workout. I had begun to suspect that Gary didn't have much confidence in Casual Lies. What with all the reports about Stanley's dietary upset, who could blame him? Gary's agent had even called to inquire about Casual Lies' condition. He explained if we weren't going to run, they could schedule to ride the older horse In Excess in New York the same weekend as the Derby.

Coupled with several other conversations we'd had with Gary, we were getting a fairly clear picture that he would only stay with Casual Lies until something better came along. I understood that—it was part of the business, and beyond that, who were we to him? He really didn't know us.

He could very easily have been buying into what the critics were saying: Shelley Riley didn't have enough experience to run a horse in the Kentucky Derby. So even though I preferred to have Jim on Stanley, we let Gary work him. We thought it was in our best interest to showcase Stanley's ability and impress Gary Stevens, who had never been on him before.

We got up at 3:30 a.m. to be sure Casual Lies was ready for his 7 a.m. workout. Gary was flying in from California on the red eye, and his flight was delayed. He wasn't sure he was going to make it.

We had arranged to work with one of Carl Nafzger's horses and had agreed to start off head and head. Carl, who had trained the 1990 Kentucky Derby winner, Unbridled, had come by our barn soon after we arrived at Churchill and

146

became a friend in short order. He was doing us a huge favor to bring out a nice horse, knowing we were going to put in a sharp workout and had no intentions of staying head and head if his horse couldn't keep up.

Carl and I felt the same way: We didn't like any of our horses to get outworked. I think it is bad for their psyches and tried to avoid that happening, as I'm sure Carl did. Nonetheless, he made it possible for Stanley to have company going five-eights, and I was grateful.

Gary arrived just in the nick of time, soon after we had tacked up Casual Lies, and I told him to be careful when he started backtracking because Casual Lies was feeling sharp again and might jump around. Sure enough, Stanley did exactly what I said he might, nearly pulling off an Arazi-Patrick Valenzuela-type move. Gary laughed at himself later, telling us he had forgotten what I had said and felt very fortunate not to have embarrassed himself by falling off in front of the whole world.

A big crowd had gathered to watch us go to the track and work. It was not as big a crowd as the one Arazi attracted, but it was certainly large enough to make me nervous after the terrible embarrassment of that maiden outworking Casual Lies when he had gotten sick.

The horses broke off together at the five-eighths pole, and Casual Lies blew away from his company at the head of the lane like the other horse was tied to a post. Stanley traveled the distance in one of the fastest times for that particular morning. Gary returned to the barn a true believer.

"I have never worked a horse that accelerated as fast as he did," he said. "When I asked him to run at the head of the lane, he just exploded. He is so powerful."

I had accomplished my main goal by letting Gary Stevens work Casual Lies. He now had confidence in my horse. It didn't matter what he thought of me. Everybody was happy now, Stanley more than anyone. My colt was electrified, bold and ready to run.

Later that day after all the hoopla had died down, we went by Arazi's barn on our way to see Carl Nafzger. Arazi's grooms were lined up along the brick wall that runs along all the shedrows, and one of the grooms was holding the most unusual pitchfork I had ever seen. Considering that I do clean stalls, I was very interested in it. I asked if I could see it, and when I got my hands on it, I loved it. It was very light, with great balance, unlike our metal and wood forks. Later someone would explain that a man in France grows a unique type of tree that he prunes and trains into the shape of either a three- or a four-prong fork.

While I was inspecting the fork, Arazi's grooms were admiring Jim's baseball cap, which was black with a sky blue rose and had "Casual Lies" embroidered on it in white script. I'd had them made up the week before, and they were the hit of the backside. I don't speak French, and they didn't speak English—it took about two minutes for us to barter fork for cap. They did drive a hard bargain, though. When I capitulated easily, they thought maybe they should try for two hats instead of one. Two fingers upheld, they got their caps, and I got Arazi's pitchfork.

~

SOCIAL EVENTS WERE REALLY cranking up around Churchill Downs, and life was becoming one big whirlwind. I didn't attend every event I was invited to because, if I had, we would have been out every night. The Kentucky Thoroughbred Breeders Awards Banquet was most definitely an event I'm glad I didn't miss. Kentucky Governor Brereton Jones and his wife attended, as did Tom Meeker, the president of Churchill Downs. It was quite an honor to meet all the dignitaries.

The awards were touching, and the introduction and short interviews with the different trainers were quite entertaining. LeRoy Jolley was very witty chatting at the podium with Chris Lincoln of the ESPN show *Thoroughbred Digest*. They played off each other and had the room roaring with laughter.

The evening gave me an insight into the horse industry from a different viewpoint. I saw this very old industry steeped in tradition, where families spanning generations had been passionately immersed in the business of breeding, selling, buying and racing Thoroughbreds. This was vastly different from my humble beginnings as a young girl, riding a massive black draft horse while he pulled the plow through the fields of sunflowers.

Allen Paulson, one of Arazi's owners, discussed winning the $5 million Triple Crown bonus sponsored by the Chrysler Corporation. This program would pay out $5 million to the owners of any horse who could win all three of the Triple Crown races. If no horse won the Triple Crown, a consolation of $1 million would go to the horse who accumulated the most bonus points and ran in all three races in the series.

As he talked, Paulson seemed pretty confident he would be collecting the $5 million bonus rather than the $1 million consolation bonus. You have to admire confidence as an asset in any business endeavor.

~

AS THE WEATHER CONTINUED to be so unpredictable, I made it my practice to head for the barn at 10 p.m. nightly, both to water off and blanket Stanley as needed. Over the years, I have visited the barn at night more times than I could count so that I could check on horses I was worried about. Quiet and peaceful, it was a nice way to cap off another busy day.

After tending to Stanley on one such night, I stepped out of the shedrow and was heading back to my car when I glanced up to admire the always beautiful twin spires perched high atop the massive grandstand. With spotlights carefully positioned to showcase their grandeur, the spires were starkly silhouetted against the velvety blackness of a cloud free sky, and on this particularly cold evening the bright white lights gave a pale blue, almost phosphorescent sheen to the spires. A mist carried on the night air passed between the spotlights and the spires, pushed along by a soft and unfelt breeze, making the image shimmer ever so slightly and giving the spires an almost ethereal quality.

Afraid to blink, I stood mesmerized, apprehensive that the beautiful image would evaporate into the night. With the spires glimmering in the distance, and the track poised in silence beneath them, all the history that had taken place here struck me viscerally. I cocked my head. Would I hear the beating of hooves, see the steam from flared nostrils as one of the greats from the past appeared out of the mist and galloped beyond my view into the darkness?

How many people and horses had come before me? They all brought so many hopes and dreams, some destined to be fulfilled while others were dashed with a slow exhale of breath. Win or lose, the memories would live on, joined into the rich history of the Downs.

I felt that press of history in the cold night as I gazed at the iconic spires and stood in awe of everything they represented. I felt more than heard the whispered promise and wondered if fate would smile on me. Would my destiny lead me to a place in the history I felt surrounding me this night?

As I drove away, my rearview mirror framed the spires glimmering through the shroud of blue mist. I was ready for the answer to my question.

~

CHURCHILL DOWNS HAS AN extremely valuable aid for the Derby participants coming from out of town called the Host Program. They pair us up with volunteers from the community to help ease the way in unfamiliar territory. We were blessed with two of the nicest people you would ever want to meet. While the Kentucky Derby experience brings out the finest in people, the very best for me came in the forms of two local attorneys, David and Lucille Fannin. When they joined the program, they actually asked for me.

Despite my best attempts, many times they were destined to receive rather short shrift from me because of the constant barrage by reporters. David and Lucille patiently waited, using up their valuable time until I could break free from yet another round of interviews or introductions going on every morning for hours on end. I recall the innumerable times they waited quietly off to the side of the throng, always smiling.

Lucille has the prettiest natural red hair, long and wavy. She had a big smile, which was always at the ready, and she was gracious, warm, intelligent and very classy—absolutely the quintessential southern lady. David was not unlike a good doctor. He made you feel like you were in capable hands, that everything would always turn out okay. He had a keen eye for details, which probably contributed greatly to his success as an attorney.

Lucille brought Stanley fresh gourmet carrots every day, tiny tender baby carrots that he ate in one bite. He started pawing the minute he spied her heading toward the barn, easy to recognize with that flaming red hair glowing in the bright Kentucky sunlight. When Lucille found I didn't have a Derby hat and didn't know where to get one (my hat size is bigger than the average woman's), she showed up the next day with a hat box containing a white hat, complete with red silk roses she had sewn on herself. She was just so charming.

Chrysler Corporation provided, along with the bonus opportunity, a brand new Chrysler New Yorker for the owners of Triple Crown contenders to drive at each event. This was a very nice touch that all of the Derby connections appreciated. The New Yorkers were white with an insignia on both front doors that designated the cars as official Chrysler Triple Crown vehicles. It didn't take us long to realize that, in these cars, we could go virtually anywhere, no questions asked, on the vast Churchill grounds. We even joked that we might get away with speeding.

On race day, the car with its insignia was as good as a police cruiser for getting through the heavy traffic. We used it to shuttle people back and forth to the grandstand, which would have been totally impossible without that car. Walking several miles around fences and barricades was the only alternative.

~

WE STAYED AT THE HOLIDAY INN Southwest while we were in Kentucky. The staff soon learned that we had a Kentucky Derby horse and did plenty of nice things for us that were above and beyond their normal protocol. They treated us like celebrities.

Since it takes me so long to get ready in the morning, I usually get up before Jim. One morning while I was engaged in the daily ritual of blow drying my hair, I became aware of a noise loud enough to be heard over the roar of the hair dryer. Jim had a significant hearing loss and had been forced to wear a bone-conduction hearing aid since his early thirties. Not wearing the hearing aid in bed, he was still sound asleep when I turned off the hair dryer to locate the source of the loud noise.

I discovered it was a fire alarm and rushed to open the door of our room. Red lights were flashing up and down the halls while the shrieking sirens blasted away. I ran back into the room and shook Jim awake. We grabbed Stanley's registration papers and the checkbook, and with shoes in hand, we ran out the door and down six flights of stairs.

I had visions of dangling from the windows by sheets. At least a hundred people milled around in the parking lot in various stages of disarray when we arrived. I glanced back up at the hotel, wondering which floor was on fire, and was astounded to see people, bare-chested or in pajamas, coming to windows here and there. They would look around for a while and then calmly walk away.

As we stood outside, the rumor began to circulate that it was a false alarm. One guest strolled by us, video camera in hand, narrating as the camera rolled: "Well, here we are in the parking lot of the Holiday Inn. All our belongings are burning up. As you can see, here is one of the numerous fire engines in attendance." There were only two fire engines, and one of those was pulling out of the parking lot.

The guy went on and on in this vein, well aware, like the rest of us now returning to our rooms, that it had been a false alarm. Jim and I laughed about how this man was creating an exciting, albeit fictional, episode for his vacation videos. What I didn't find funny was my frazzled half-dried hair and no cosmetics. I would have to face the media all morning feeling unkempt and half dressed without my makeup.

That same day, both Karl Schmitt and Buck Wheat asked

if I would mind joining several other guests on the Van Vance radio talk show on WHAS AM 840, to be broadcast that evening. His radio program was broadcast nationwide at 50,000 watts of power, something Karl and Buck fortunately failed to mention or I would have been nervous. Buck picked us up that evening and drove us to the station in downtown Louisville. Karl met us there and led the lamb to slaughter.

The studio was an acoustical room with a horse shoe-shaped table. There was seating around the perimeter for about five people. Each of these five stations had a headphone and a microphone attached to a mechanical swing arm, not unlike something you might see in a dentist's office for holding the drill. Van sat in the center of the horseshoe, surrounded by all his equipment. His technical support group could be seen in the next room through a huge soundproofed window.

Once the show started and we were on the air, Van talked a bit with each of the guests in the studio, introducing us and making us feel at ease. He also had several guests who joined in the discussions via telephone. My experience with Van Vance was very positive. He had the ability as a talk show host to voice an opinion without coming across too strongly. He skillfully manipulated his guests to entertain his audience, encouraging us to voice our own opinions. He allowed rebuttals and somehow managed to keep us fairly friendly despite our differences. We pushed the edges a few times, especially when Mister Opinion himself, Andy Beyer, phoned in.

Andy was a handicapper who had developed his own gimmick to handicap races. He tended to be quite vocal in his picks and pans, and his summaries on the horses' chances definitely tended toward the hurtful side. He didn't like Casual Lies, his chances or his connections, and to that end his remarks tended to be quite catty and cutting. If someone had told me he would be taking part, I might have passed on the talk show. I loved Stanley—he was the best thing that ever happened to me. To have Beyer say unkind or hurtful things about my horse to help sell a handicapping gimmick was painful.

The ultimate test of handicapping is to put your money where your mouth is. Many different handicapping opinions and Derby selections were heard over the air that evening, and despite Andy Beyer, I found it interesting and quite entertaining to be part of a program broadcast throughout the country.

~

I HAD BECOME INCREASINGLY superstitious since the start of this fantastic episode in my life. I spent so much time knocking on wood that it was amazing my hand had not begun to resemble a splintered piece of firewood.

One morning on our way to get our Kentucky racing licenses, we had parked in front of the Kentucky Racing Commission structure in the Churchill Downs barn area. As I gathered up my purse, I looked out the windshield and saw what appeared to be a Treasury bill on the grass directly in front of the car.

The wind had been kicking up all morning and was gusting pretty hard by that time. My gaze was glued to this piece of paper as one end lifted up with each gust that hit it. It certainly appeared to be green and sure looked like the real thing. There it rested, curling up, almost like it was beckoning to me. This was an omen if I ever saw one.

Jim was asking me a question, but I didn't answer. My eyes were riveted to the spot as I opened the car door. I crept up on my own personal omen, when a particularly strong gust of wind lifted it fully two-thirds off the ground. Fluttering as if it had its own green gossamer wings, I was sure this $20 bill—I was now close enough to see its denomination—was going to skitter away before I could capture it. Just before another gust took it away, I pounced, reaching down, managing to grasp the Treasury bill in my fist. Exultant, I turned and looked at Jim, who stared at me from the car in wonder as I danced around in the grass. He was sure I had finally gone over the edge. I waved the $20 at him triumphantly.

"You know what this means, don't you?" I asked as he joined me. Not waiting for an answer, I continued, "It means no matter what, we will not leave Kentucky empty-handed."

We laughed together and proudly showed it all over the racing commission office—our omen of good luck to come. No one claimed that $20, and I still have it today.

~

MORE AND MORE WISHES FOR our success arrived daily in the form of telegrams, letters and phone messages. I wanted to thank everyone who sent these to us. We were touched and grateful. They meant a lot, and I have saved every one. At one point, someone sent a single rose to us at the track, delivered to the barn by one of the security guards. I put it in a white Styrofoam cup on the ledge in front of Stanley's stall. A single crimson exclamation—the regal blossom which symbolized the great race we all coveted so badly.

Two bouquets of roses were sent to me at the hotel. They were beautiful and were the first thing I saw when I woke up each morning and the last thing before turning the lights off at night.

It was getting increasingly hard to get up in the morning. Invitations came in for some sort of gala or party every night.

Besides the Kentucky Thoroughbred Breeders Awards Banquet, the press party at the Galt House was the only other event we agreed to attend. Located in a massive convention room, the party included lavish and plentiful food beyond our wildest imaginations. The center of the room was dominated by a huge assortment of tables adorned with lovely ice sculptures that were arranged like glittering statuary.

Huge prawns cascaded down a mountain of ice in several places on this oasis of food, while many varieties of cheese, fruit and crackers completed the layout. Around the periphery of the room were several mint julep stations, where the traditional Derby drink was being served in the official Derby No. 118 glasses. If you tried to drink a sufficient number of these very strong drinks to acquire a complete set of Derby glasses, it undoubtedly would not have ended well. I surreptitiously poured my mint juleps into water glasses and was able to walk out under my own power at the end of the evening.

Chefs served roasted meats with all the trimmings at other food stations throughout this vast room. They had a huge pot of a local stew called Kentucky Burgoo, which I loved. When I enquired what was in it, a native Kentuckian laughed and replied, "Everything plus road kill." I swallowed rather loudly while looking into the depths of the pot suspiciously. I didn't see anything recognizable.

The dessert bar was nearly my undoing. Not much of a drinker, I am more often than not the designated driver, and I will often quip, "I can't get arrested for eating and driving." As we waddled to the parking lot at the end of the evening, I was glad Buck Wheat had been kind enough to drive us to and from our destination yet again.

I would have been far more careful about what I was seen

eating if I had known so many people were interested in the things owners of Derby horses ate. The next day there was a rumor going around about Jenny Craig, who had attended a party in the old paddock at Churchill Downs, one of many events that we skipped. Several reporters said she was seen going through the buffet line twice, her plate piled high with pork ribs.

Oh for heaven's sake, that was totally ridiculous, and I found it almost too funny for words. I wonder what was rumored about me. "Shelley Riley seen with two, count 'em, two pieces of Derby pie, while she left with six empty Derby glasses clutched in her arms."

~

TWO DAYS HELD GREATER importance to us than any others while we were in Kentucky. Derby Day was the most important, obviously, while the second was entry day. Entry day included the Derby draw, when post positions for the race would be determined. With a very large field expected and need for a second, auxiliary starting gate becoming almost certain, nothing could have been more important to us than the post position we drew.

Luck of the draw is an oft-used phrase in horse racing, and we had our fingers and toes crossed that morning as we headed over to the Kentucky Derby Museum. Nobody should ever visit Louisville without a trip to the Kentucky Derby Museum.

Churchill Downs had set up a terrific tribute, not only to the Kentucky Derby, but also to the entire sport of racing. The museum abounds with interesting and entertaining exhibits, literally something for everyone, including some very fine equine art. A slide presentation on a surround screen filled the oval-shaped second-floor balcony above our heads.

As we stood gathered for the draw of arguably the most important three-year-old race in the world, the room darkened and the slide show began. It was accompanied by a narration with music and other sounds so well selected that it virtually came to life before our rapt gazes.

The show started with the crisp greens and blues of a Kentucky morning and the birds singing the dawn chorus. The sounds of the foaling barn as a new life comes dropping into the anxiously waiting hands of the attendants. The bang of the starting gate, the jockeys yelling at one another, the sound of hooves pounding into the dirt and the crack of an encouraging whip all brought our pulse rates up, along with goose bumps and a prickle to the back of the neck.

Under the circumstances for which we had all gathered, the story being depicted high above our heads was just so profound, so personal. I stood mesmerized, my breath held in check—I watched and listened with a growing fervor as the presentation built to its final crescendo: "And down the stretch they come," rang the voice of Dave Johnson throughout the room. There was a moment of absolute silence—the atmosphere in the room was thick with emotion. We'd all been served up a glimpse of a very real possibility, one that awaited each of us who had dared to dream and come this far.

As the majority of us dabbed surreptitiously at our eyes, the Kentucky Derby draw began. The mechanics of the draw were fairly simple. All the horses were entered on official entry blanks. Each entry blank contained the date and race number, the horse's name, his owner and trainer, the colors of the silks, the weight carried by the horse and the jockey's name.

The entry blanks were used in conjunction with

numbered pills, roughly the size of marbles, which represented the post-position numbers. These pills were round and white, with one flat side on which a number had been engraved. They would be dropped into a leather bottle with a neck so narrow only one pill could pass through at a time.

After all the Derby horses' names were read aloud, the entry blanks were shuffled thoroughly and placed in the entry box. The entry box was more like an upright slot, with the horses' names on the entry blanks facing away from the person drawing. As one person removed a number from the bottle, another person simultaneously drew one entry blank. Everything possible had been done to ensure the integrity of the draw.

The post I dreaded more than any other was the one hole. With two starting gates joined in a single line and the narrowness of the track, the horse in the first post must break and immediately angle his stride to the right to avoid riding the inside rail. The ideal post positions would be five through nine. As the names kept coming and the better posts began to be taken, my heart beat louder and harder until it was just pounding. I felt like I do when the horses are coming down the stretch.

It seemed like an eternity, and still my horse's name had not been called. I had lost track of all the numbers, but I was pretty sure the majority of what was left would be in the auxiliary gate on the far outside. At the point when I was verging on despair, "Casual Lies" was drawn with the number three pill. Such relief washed over me that I was left weak-kneed and more than a little sick to my stomach.

The majority of the favorites ended up in the auxiliary gate, which I must admit didn't hurt my feelings any. One of the drawbacks to our post was the amount of time it would take to load that many horses in the gate. The horse with the number one post would have to stand there a very long time, for example, and before that time ended, he might rear up, turn his head into the gateman, stumble, crouch, try to break through the front of the gate, sit on the tailgate, flip or just become too calm and be flat-footed when the gate sprang open.

, The other problem is that everybody would be driving for the rail, tightening things up on the inside horses very quickly. I would have preferred the seven, eight or even the number nine post position, but at this point I was simply relieved the draw was over.

I had just spent $10,000 to see my horse's name on an overnight sheet. There would be no refund if we didn't start in the race.

Quite a large press gathering amassed in the courtyard after the draw, with Arazi's trainer, Francois Boutin, the center of attention. I can only imagine the ordeal that man must have been going through. Surely he must have been worried about his horse at this point—what with the way Arazi was training. And yet, Boutin had his game face in place as he fielded the deluge of reporters' questions.

My entourage and I all wore our Casual Lies caps and enjoyed the sun, flowers and sights in the courtyard. As this year's oddity, I still attracted plenty of attention. It was, however, a blink of the eye compared to the amount of time reporters focused on Boutin, and at this point I didn't even mind when they asked, "Surely, you can't seriously hope to outrun Arazi."

I can remember vividly how Lynn Swann entertained us in the courtyard with a complete call of the Kentucky Derby from start to finish. He was bent over riding and whipping, and he never missed a name. Of course, he had us winning.

Hey, the sun was shining, we had just got lucky with our post position draw, and our horse was feeling great. Casual Lies was one happy camper. He was affectionate, alert, cheerful and mischievous. He was playful and cavorted around every time we took him out of the stall. Our jockey now believed in my horse. I was filled with confidence that we were going to win the Kentucky Derby. It was as simple as that. Let the rest believe what they may.

~

WE LEFT THE MUSEUM WITH the intention of shopping for souvenirs and could see we wouldn't have to walk far to do it. Local vendors had set up their wares just outside the admission gates, and the variety of items they were peddling was monumental. As we headed out, we ran into Gary Stevens heading in. He was grinning from ear to ear and professed his confidence was every bit as high as ours. He was still remembering Stanley's excellent workout.

Among other things, I bought a pair of reflective eyeglasses that had the Kentucky Derby 118 logo on the lenses. I loved them and couldn't wait to wear them for the photographers the next time they all showed up while we were out grazing Stanley. I was surprised and more than a little disappointed when one of the photographers asked me to lose the glasses. He said it made me look like a tourist. I suppose that was better than the TV people, who kept saying that my dark glasses made me look like a drug dealer. I had never seen anyone who looked like me on *Miami Vice* being hauled off for drug dealing. Nonetheless, somebody was always asking me to take my glasses off. It's a good thing they weren't prescription, but still, I was left squinting into the camera with a perpetual frown in the bright Kentucky sun.

162

While our oddity quotient was rising, our underdog status was skyrocketing through the roof. I was being asked for autographs and could hardly believe the number of people who wanted to have their picture taken with me. I was constantly posing with my arm around strangers. A very large portion of these people were grooms, exercise boys and girls, pony people, hot walkers and other women trainers. Bumper stickers had been printed up by one of the local organizations, and the Casual Lies stickers were the first to sell out. I didn't even get one.

I gave away more than $400 worth of Casual Lies caps before I ran out. The vendor who drove his van around selling caps was inundated with requests for Casual Lies caps, and he sold out in one day. Well-wishers came by the barn daily. They all professed the desire to see the little guy beat the boys with the big bucks. Americans love the "pull yourself up by your bootstraps" saga, and I certainly personified that story.

I went from my first Heinz 57 saddle horse to running in the Kentucky Derby with my first stakes horse as a trainer. I had even bought him with borrowed money. I still had my ticket to ride and had never anticipated a destination so eagerly, and yet with so much anxiety, as the one that lay ahead.

Chapter Eleven

Kentucky Derby Day

No other race carries the weight of so much history as does the Kentucky Derby. Ask a stranger, "What does the word 'Derby' bring to mind?" The most common response would be, "The Kentucky Derby." This single race is an event of such scope that the Commonwealth of Kentucky seems to host its own mini world's fair every year, complete with color and pageantry. The enthusiastic involvement of the people of Kentucky, both in horse racing and out, has been instrumental in helping to evolve the occasion into the extravaganza for the senses that it has become today.

To be there for the event was truly a joy. To be one of the participants was an opportunity so wondrous I could barely comprehend it, and I struggled to embrace the reality. I was about to saddle a horse in the Kentucky Derby when just a few years before I considered myself lucky if a horse I owned could break his maiden in the lowest claiming races at the Fresno fair. But racing is so much more than just winning purse money. Millions of people would be watching the Derby on television, and quite a few viewers would be rooting for their favorite underdogs, which included Stanley and me. There is a lot of emotion involved in racing, and at this level it was colossal.

The day of days, Saturday, May 2, 1992, began at 3:30 a.m. for Jim and me. Having been warned about the legendary traffic on Derby Day, we were up earlier than usual after a restless night. We gathered everything we needed for the day, knowing there would be no coming back to the room.

We certainly weren't the only ones up early. As we traveled through the normally quiet residential streets near the track, they were abuzz with activity. The locals readied their properties to take every advantage of the opportunity the Kentucky Derby offered every year. Hand-painted parking signs abounded as residents prepared to park cars in their garages, driveways and even on their lawns for large fees. Refreshment stands were springing up in front of several homes, with everything from bottled water to hush puppies for sale.

As expected, Stanley was still sleeping when we arrived at the barn. We tried not to disturb him, whispering quietly to our guard, but he sensed our arrival and got up with a rustle of hay and a soft nicker of greeting. Casual Lies is a talker, and he never failed to greet us, no matter what time of day it was.

After we fed him, we continued our chat with the security guard over donuts and coffee. We talked about the night's events and a little about the day ahead. We respected our security guards and left the tack room open for them to sit inside in the cold of night. They rewarded us with friendship and a devotion to our horse. They liked Stanley, and they liked us.

Once Stanley finished his grain, he was pushing against his stall webbing, anticipating our morning wrestling match. I would try to put his halter on over his busy mouth while he successfully foiled each attempt. The halter always ended up in his mouth despite my best efforts, and then he would refuse to let go. This would go on for several minutes until

Jim finally put a hand on Stanley's muzzle to distract him. This little game was harmless enough, and while I didn't always enjoy it, Stanley certainly did.

Next I brushed him thoroughly, and Stanley switched his attention to getting the brushes in his mouth. He was very quick, and once he had the brush clenched in his teeth, it became an outright tug-of-war contest.

Some would say I spoiled him, but I didn't care. I spoiled all my horses as long as they didn't take advantage and try to hurt me or end up hurting themselves. I don't see why a racehorse can't just be a horse once in a while.

After we finished brushing and wrestling, Stanley would normally be walked by Jim for an hour about the shedrow or else would go to the track. Today he would walk. As far as Stanley knew, it was just another day. We would endeavor to keep him thinking that way for as long as possible to ensure a restful morning for all concerned.

On any race day, at some point Stanley would realize that lunch wasn't forthcoming and start getting suspicious. If the evening feeding time rolled around without his gourmet meal arriving, he would get downright angry. When he heard the rattle of feed tubs up and down the shedrow and didn't receive his meal, he'd rear, strike and do zoomies around his stall, peppering the wall with his hind hooves. That would certainly garner the attention he was asking for, and fortunately I always got to him before he could hurt himself.

All trainers I know draw their horses to some extent the day of the race. Drawing means to withhold a certain portion of that day's ration until after the race. The thinking is that horses can't compete as well with a stomach full of partially digested food.

Unfortunately for Stanley, good horses almost always run late in the day, generally right about their normal dinnertime. Being creatures of habit, they can get quite irritated when denied their food. Since Stanley was usually bedded on rice hulls, we didn't have to muzzle him on race day to keep him from grazing around in the bedding while looking for scraps. Once he figured out all the food was gone after his midmorning feeding, he would look around for a while and then give up and go to sleep.

Since he was now bedded on timothy hay, I knew we were facing a very long day with a cantankerous horse. Stanley doesn't like timothy, but if there wasn't anything else, he would certainly chow down on it. So we would be forced to tie him up in his stall or muzzle him. Although he's fine tied up as long as you stand there with him, I didn't plan on standing there for six hours, nor did I want him to either.

If you really wanted to see a petulant Casual Lies, put a muzzle on him. He would try to rub it off, shake it off or smash it off. He was relentless—he never gave up. If you walked up to him when he had a muzzle on, you had better have an arm up to protect yourself, because he would whap you upside the head with the muzzle to demonstrate his discontent. Therefore, when the time would come to stop his eating, I would have to figure a way to keep Stanley entertained and food-free until race time without muzzling him or tying him up.

~

THE EARLY MORNING HOURS on Derby day turned out to be remarkably quiet compared to the previous days. I think the media had filed all of their stories complete with their picks and pans. It was now put up or shut up time for all concerned.

Churchill Downs opens the stable area on Kentucky Derby Day to their employees and their families for picnicking. We found that we were now at ground zero of the most popular tourist attraction on the backside. Row after row of people would line up at the various barricades pointing and yelling. I was amazed at how loud some of the people were. Here we were trying to keep things peaceful for our athlete, and suddenly it felt like we were an exhibit at a county fair or the major attraction at a carnival side show. I tried to answer all their questions in the beginning, but it soon became apparent that this would go on all day.

Finally, I was forced to position myself in front of Stanley's stall in a chair with a book. I had my back to the crowd to keep them from lobbing questions over the barricades at the top of their lungs. Stanley liked this. He nibbled at my toes, knees or fingers—whatever he could reach. This strategy kept Stanley entertained for a while so that he wasn't grazing through the timothy hay bedding in his stall, and it seemed to quiet the crowd to some extent. Our day guard certainly earned his money keeping the sightseers behind the barricades. As the day progressed, things finally started to heat up—and not just the weather.

A producer from ABC television came by asking for an on-air interview with Charlsie Cantey and inquired if I would be willing to wear a microphone during the entire Kentucky Derby telecast. I agreed to the first and declined the second. I didn't know what I might say during the race, and I certainly didn't want to do it on a live broadcast heard by millions around the world.

Two stretch limos pulled up, parking beside the barn near A.P. Indy's stall with their engines running. I can only assume they did this to keep the air conditioning on for the occupants. No one got out, and they seemed prepared to stay there until race time.

Neil Drysdale was still in his tackroom at the other end of

our barn after being forced, unfortunately, to scratch A.P. Indy from the Derby due to injury. When he finally got fed up, I saw him stomp out to the limos and ask them to either move or turn off their engines. Apparently the cars were pumping out carbon monoxide right into Neil's stalls. The drivers pulled away almost before he had stepped back into his shedrow. I don't know where they ended up, but it was a long way away from Neil's end of our barn.

David and Lucille Fannin, my official volunteer Kentucky Derby hosts, were a godsend on Derby Day. They tirelessly ran back and forth from the grandstand—no easy task considering the huge crowd—with paddock passes and information. They greeted all of our California friends who came to see the Derby and support us. David and Lucille made sure they found their assigned seats as well as the luncheon buffet and the saddling paddock. On a very stress-filled day, our hosts went out of their way to take a big load off my shoulders and onto their own.

Despite my good intentions and my best efforts not to think about what lay ahead, my thoughts kept returning to that corner of my mind where all the "what ifs" about the forthcoming Derby dwelt. Winning meant glory, wealth, pride and happiness, among other things. Losing obviously meant overwhelming disappointment but, above all else, ridicule and self-doubt. In those few hours left before our destiny would be revealed on Saturday, May 2, I wanted very badly for it to be Sunday, May 3.

~

AS THE DAY WORE ON, I maintained my vigil while seated in front of Stanley's stall, book in hand, rereading the same page over and over again as thoughts on winning the Derby were besieged by deep-seated uncertainty and apprehension.

Napping with his head suspended over my lap, Stanley was peaceful and unaware of my inner turmoil, and I needed to keep it that way.

The hours and minutes crawled by, and the day continued to grow hotter and hotter, the humidity going off the charts. Stanley and I were sharing his stall fan when a stiff breeze came up that provided absolutely no relief from the sweltering heaviness of the air. Track officials came by with last-minute instructions for gathering the horses prior to departing for the saddling paddock. There would not be a stop in a receiving barn as we were accustomed to in California.

Our cast of helpers assembled, and we began to prepare our horse and ourselves. Everybody, equine and human, must be buff polished and ready to put their best foot or hoof forward. Many eyes would be turned to Kentucky this day, very nearly the eyes of the world, in fact. Stanley would leave his stall shining like a new wax job.

When the 20-minute call came, the call to leave the barn, we were ready. As Casual Lies left the stall and took his first step toward our shared future, however, I was nearly overcome by a wave of fear. A realization drove all thoughts save one from my mind: not only was I walking beside a horse—*my* horse—he was just minutes away from running in the Kentucky Derby.

After leaving the barn, we approached the staging area where the horses were to gather prior to stepping onto the track. I was completely aghast at what we encountered. There was a large crowd and parked cars blocking our way.

Everybody was yelling and screaming, and most of them had their backs to us. Our pony girl, mounted on her horse, was able to spot a path between the cars, although it was filled with people. There must have been hundreds gathered here, and we had no alternative but to push an opening through them.

The pony girl started forward. A groom we had hired for the day was tucked in behind her with Casual Lies' lead shank firmly in his hand. Jim was at Stanley's left side just behind the groom, and Carl Nafzger's assistant trainer, Bryan, was a little farther back, protecting our flank. I was at Stanley's head on the right side, and our day guard from the barn was behind me. The guard would be accompanying the horse as far as the track, at which point his job would be done for another year.

There we stood with no way to make forward progress. We started yelling, "Derby horse, Derby horse, please let us through!" Because the crowd was so noisy, we couldn't be heard above the din. Suddenly, the people directly in front of us began to step aside. Unfortunately, that's when we saw a car backing directly into us through the crowd. I began to fear for my horse's safety. And there was the danger facing all these jubilant people pressing close to the Derby contenders, who do kick just like other horses.

Pounding on the trunk of the car, we got the attention of the driver but only after we had given up what few feet of real estate we had managed to cover. I was outraged that this could be happening. Where were the uniformed guards? Why wasn't there a roped-off area for these volatile horses to pass through unmolested?

I stepped forward with my arms extended and started nudging people to the side, yelling, "Please let the Derby horse through, please."

With a great deal of difficulty, I managed to get a few of the people to notice us and move aside long enough to make our way into the bowels of the crowd. We were now locked into a gauntlet, winding through the parked cars as we tried to push our way to the racetrack entrance. Happy fans were screaming and laughing, calling out to their favorite Derby horses as they passed, only inches separating the horses and handlers from the waving arms of admirers.

The pressure from the crowd was constant as we crept through—we were literally holding people back with one arm and bracing ourselves against Casual Lies with the other. I knew there were horses in front of us and behind us, but I could neither see nor hear them. The whites of Stanley's eyes were showing, and his nostrils were flared. I tried to comfort him with my voice, but he could not hear me above the melee. I placed a hand on his nostrils so he could smell me, and he seemed to settle a little.

The crowd would surge forward with each horse that passed, trying to see the next in line. We pushed back against the people, and Stanley kept his cool, barely. He started turning his head to seek the hand I held up, as if he were checking to be sure I was still there with him. How no one got hurt, I'll never know.

Finally, we reached the track—and it was like coming out of a tunnel. What a relief, I thought, yet that relief was very short-lived.

We entered the backstretch chute on the track and turned left into the clubhouse turn as we progressed toward the grandstand and saddling paddock. The crowd on the turn instantly took up where the other crowd of people had left off, but these fans were safely behind a fence and weren't as jam-packed. However, their numbers increased significantly farther around the turn until all we could see was a mass of faces on both sides of the track. The infield was a carpet of humanity.

When the throng of spectators spotted the horses coming, they started to cheer. It was awe inspiring to pass by the people calling to us from both sides of the track, and we had yet to reach the multitude of celebratory fans packed in the gigantic grandstand with its beautiful twin spires looming above.

The cheering ahead of us swelled in volume as our parade of Derby horses advanced. The noise spread from one end to the other of the vast clubhouse and grandstand structure, increasing in intensity until it seemed we were engulfed in the din. From every angle, we witnessed arms waving programs, papers, banners and hats, everything in bright colors. A face would swim out of the mass, momentarily coming into focus, and then be lost once again as we passed by. We saw friendly faces and heard friendly voices, and not one negative comment did we hear.

"Go get 'em, Stanley!"

"Hey, there's Casual Lies."

"Way to go, Shelley, win one for the girls!"

"There's Technology—where's Arazi?"

This was beyond my wildest expectations. All the happy people seemed beyond joyous, beyond ecstatic, very nearly frenzied—the magnitude of their emotions is burnt into my memory. Clearly, they had their favorites, but nonetheless they were aware of every one of us as a character playing his or her part in their enjoyment of the day.

The wind was blowing so hard that unless your hat was cemented on, you had to hold it firmly in place. Before leaving the barn with Stanley, I had picked up the lovely hat Lucille had brought for me and considered wearing it but fortunately decided not to. Besides the wind, it seemed inappropriate for me to be trying to bend over pulling the overgirth tight on my horse while worrying about whether my chapeau would get knocked to the ground. It would also undoubtedly get trampled underfoot, leaving me standing there with severe hat head for the whole world to see.

The heat had been building throughout the day, but now it was nearly unbearable. Because the forecast had called for drenching downpours, the track superintendent had not put much water on the surface to tighten it. The track was getting drier every minute the hot wind blew across it, and walking on it, I felt it was very heavy.

Think about running along the water's edge at the beach versus the dry, deep sand the water fails to reach. We call this a cuppy track, and it would be very slow and tiring on the horses. My shoes had become filled with sand after the first few steps onto the track. I should have worn boots.

By now I was regretting my black wool-knit suit. Born and raised in the dry warmth of California, I didn't handle humidity well and wasn't adapting as I'd hoped I would. Moreover, walking in this deep sand was an ordeal—I felt my leg muscles tying up as Stanley and I trudged through it.

At last we turned left onto the path that would take us under the grandstand and through the tunnel into the saddling paddock. It was like stepping up onto pavement after the sandbox condition of the racetrack. As we left the tunnel and entered the paddock, we couldn't see anything but more people. Everybody seemed to be having a ball, although I don't know how. They were so crammed in together that they couldn't move other than to wave arms and clutch colorful hats to keep them from blowing away.

Within the confines of the crowded saddling paddock was the crème de la crème of horse racing society. It looked as if the dress code was fashioned after high season at Epsom or Ascot in England. The massive crowd must have been an absolute nightmare for the bodyguards with the M. C. Hammer and Sheikh Maktoum camps.

Some fans had climbed onto the wrought iron fencing

close to the stall assigned to Arazi and kept calling out, "Hey! Hey, Maktoum, turn this way." No response from the sheikh. Finally, after repeatedly calling out in this manner, they tried, "Yo, Maktoum Baby. Hey, Maktoum Baby, turn this way."

That worked. He finally turned, smiled slightly and shook his head. I couldn't help but wonder what would have been the outcome if a few of his subjects in Dubai had addressed him as "Yo, Maktoum Baby."

I paid very little attention to what was being said, other than that humorous blast at the sheikh. I was still trying to keep up with my horse as he was led around the walk ring in the saddling paddock by his groom. I was hoping my presence would help keep him calm, but finally I just had to stop. I felt like a parboiled red potato and had to find a way to cool off. My face was pounding with each beat of my heart. Jim and I seldom eat or even think to drink on race day. The lack of fluid intake this day was proving to be a very big mistake. My mouth felt like it was full of Elmer's Glue.

The valet showed up with the tack, and we saddled a wound-up hairy stick of dynamite. Casual Lies was more than ready now—he was about to explode. Suddenly, the jockeys emerged from the throng surrounding us, and Gary Stevens sidled up to us in our assigned stall with a big smile. He seemed calm and cool. I liked his demeanor, but all the same I was grateful when I heard the call for "riders up." I wanted out of this crowded paddock before Stanley got hurt by another horse acting out.

Up went the riders and my job was over, at least from the trainer's standpoint. The hard part was about to begin. Now that I didn't have to stay calm for the sake of my horse, I could give in to the nerves. Already breathless, I put one foot in front of the other as I followed my new friends David and

Lucille Fannin.

We filed out of the saddling paddock and found a huge group of owners, trainers, dignitaries, family and friends lined up to enter a narrow stairway that provided the only access to the upper grandstand, where our seats where located.

While I waited my turn in the single-file line, I missed seeing Casual Lies step onto the track, missed the magic moment of hearing "My Old Kentucky Home" played as my horse paraded to the wonderful melody. Seeing and hearing this never failed to give me goose bumps and bring tears to my eyes when I watched at home every year. In some ways, it was almost the best part of the event. To this day, I still regret missing that moment when the band started up and the crowd joined in, singing along.

While Jim and I continued to wait in line, the thought that we might not even get to see the race struck me with alarm. My stress level continued to climb as time seemed to fly by. We crept to the top of the stairs and then rushed down hallways and around corners. We ran right past officials who wanted to see passes and tickets. Jim and I followed David and Lucille blindly. Without them, we would never have reached the seats in time, premium seats that owners and trainers are required to pay for to see their three-year-olds run on the first Saturday in May.

We stepped into our box and barely had time to position ourselves before the horses approached the gate. I was so nervous that I hadn't been thinking very much about the race. I was trying very hard to catch my breath and calm down so that, hopefully, I would be standing when the race was over.

The physical pain I'd had before other races was a deep one in my chest this time, and it seemed to be pushing down my left arm. People were talking to me, but I don't think I was responding. Everyone was dripping wet, and the high humidity felt like a sauna.

I wanted this race to be over more than I had ever wanted anything in my life. While waiting what seemed like an eternity for the huge field to be loaded, I confronted all my worst fears, piling more stress onto an already overloaded cart.

What if he got left in the gate?

What if the field closed up in front of him?

What if he clipped heels?

What if he got hurt in this cavalry charge?

One thing for sure, there was nothing I could do to help Casual Lies now. My horse was in the hands of Gary Stevens, a man I barely knew. I could only hope that he would take advantage of every opportunity, overcome each adversity and have more confidence in Casual Lies than he did in us.

When the horses were all in the starting gate, we could barely see any of them or the track. The view from the seats was certainly not what we had expected.

Bang! The gate opened, and the horses were on their way in the 118th running of the Kentucky Derby. More than 137,000 people were on their feet, screaming at the top of their lungs.

The roar was monumental when the horses pounded down the stretch for the first time. As I waited for the field to come into sight from behind the columns blocking my view of nearly everything on the track, I listened to the thundering beat of my heart. It seemed as if the top of my head might lift right off.

And so—just like that, the clock had started to tick on the most important two minutes of my life. When the horses swept down the stretch into view, I could see the pack angling toward the rail. The jockeys were maneuvering the thousands of pounds of horseflesh for position into the first turn, the most dangerous part of the race.

Rounding the first turn, the crowded field made it difficult for me to recognize Casual Lies, and I couldn't hear the call of the race over the screaming crowd and pounding of my heart. I could see he was neither in front nor last, however, and those were both good things.

Although I completely lost sight of Casual Lies down the backstretch, I was grateful for the white headstall on his bridle. It at least narrowed down the number of horses to follow. Jim turned and reassured me that Stanley was in good position.

I strained, I prayed, I begged, please...please...please be okay. Suddenly Casual Lies emerged from a tightly packed bunch surging around the final turn for home. I could see his beautiful head, his bright white headstall. He was going for the lead. I nearly went to my knees when he pulled away from the field, opening up daylight. It looked like he was going to win for fun as he widened the distance between him and the mass of horses strung out behind him.

"Come on, Stanley, you can do it, big boy," I whispered, and then I wailed and screamed like the multitude around me, as if by sheer volume we could bring him home. Over the deafening noise, I could make out Jim yelling his heart out, something he never did. But I could also see that Stanley was looking around, pricking his ears, thinking there was nothing else to outrun. He couldn't see Lil E. Tee blowing up out of nowhere, but then, that was his jockey's responsibility.

When Gary saw Lil E. Tee coming by on the outside fast enough to win, he rode hard for the money. Stanley tried to regain his momentum and managed to pull back some ground, but it was too late. The race was over, and the moment was past. History had passed us by, and the wonderful moment of winning belonged to another. I was devastated and completely drained.

With nothing left to hold me up, I went to sit down, but someone had folded the chairs to give us more room for jumping around. I would have been sitting unceremoniously on the concrete floor of the box if helping hands hadn't rescued me. I simply had no strength left to save myself. A chair was found, and I was helped out of my sweater. Someone went for water, while another friend fanned me with a program.

I just wanted to be left alone to cry and suffer. Jim was frightened. I must have looked a sight, bright red and soaking wet huddled up in a chair while crying my heart out over a lost opportunity. Jim hovered, stricken, asking me if I was all right.

"We lost!" I blubbered.

"It's okay, he ran big, he ran a huge second," Jim said, trying to comfort me.

"I wanted to win."

Jim chuckled softly as he took my hand. "Shelley, we just ran second in the Kentucky Derby!"

It took a few minutes to pull myself together and realize the significance of what he was saying—that there is no shame in running second in the greatest three-year-old race in the world. It may not have been as good as first, but it was good all the same. Casual Lies' effort had made us proud as never before, and most important of all, he was safe. He would not have to face the risks of running in a 19-horse field ever again.

While I was very disappointed at that moment, I would be ecstatic later. There is winning, and there is losing. Anything worse than first is losing, right? Before the Derby, I would have said yes to that, but no, not now. Even last in the Kentucky Derby is not losing. Losers do not make it to the Kentucky Derby in the first place.

~

WHEN I WAS ABLE, I STARTED down the stairs heading back to the barn to find my horse and give him the attention he deserved. But up popped Lucille. A reception was being held in the Kentucky Derby Museum after the race. It was expected that we would be there. I was torn. I wanted to go to my horse. After all, we hadn't won, and wasn't this the winner's party?

Not at all, this reception was for us as well, and all our friends from California were there. Lucille said everybody would be disappointed if I didn't go. Finally I was convinced it would be bad form on my part not to show up. So once again I found myself following David and Lucille. For the first time ever I wasn't at the barn before Stanley was completely cooled out. Jim reassured me that he would go back and make sure everything was in order before he joined us.

Frankly, I'm not sure I could have walked back to the barn right then anyway; my knees were still shaking. With my hair hanging in a wet mass, I ran my fingers through it, trying desperately to give it a semblance of order as I followed along behind my temporary host. I was pretty sure every iota of my makeup had washed away and that my face was red and blotchy from crying. I felt puffy and raw physically as well as emotionally.

Disheveled and uncomfortable, I approached the museum, and as luck would have it, I ran into a jubilant Steve Haskin. He stopped in front of me, eyes brilliant, grinning from ear to ear.

"You did it," he chortled.

I frowned at him. "Steve, we lost."

Stunned, he stood there for a moment taking in the look on my face. "Shelley, you just did something no other woman has done in the entire history of the Kentucky Derby. You ran second."

I blinked, thought about that for a moment, and replied, "Really? Oh my!"

That certainly gave me a whole new perspective on my horse's courageous race. Up to that point, I hadn't given the female trainer perspective much thought, at least as far as any finish other than first. I certainly knew that a horse trained by a woman had never won the race. I didn't know that I was only the sixth woman to saddle a horse in the 118-year history of the Kentucky Derby and that second was by far the best finish.

Armed with this thought, I joined the party in the museum. My friends from California pounced on me the minute I came in the door. They were all so excited about our finish, and I must admit it became infectious.

I basked in their enthusiasm while reminding myself that Casual Lies had just given all he had after getting sick and coming very close to missing his one and only opportunity to compete in the Kentucky Derby. He had fought his way through an illness that had cost him more than a week of very valuable training time. Despite that huge setback, my gallant horse had run us both into the history books. My disappointment was slowly turning to wonder and a huge sense of accomplishment.

It was exciting to be there with all the people, winners included. Chris Lincoln from ESPN introduced me to Pat Day, the winning jockey. Pat squinted up at me and seemed confused at the mention of my name.

"You know, Pat, Casual Lies," Chris prompted.

"Casual Ties?" Pat said, frowning mightily and mulling it over. Suddenly his face cleared and he brightened. Before turning away and dismissing us out of hand, he said, "Oh yes, nice little horse."

Chris seemed embarrassed, and I was amused. As I watched Pat walk away, I thought, "That was good for me—certainly keeps everything in the proper perspective."

~

DURING THE RECEPTION, THE skies had opened up, and it was absolutely a deluge outside. Casual Lies was safely tucked back in his stall when I got back to the barn after trudging through the rain. He was content with a bag of hay, and he seemed nonetheless worse for wear. He nickered softly as I approached. He seemed as glad to see me as I was to see him, only this time rather than grab for my fingers, he rested his muzzle in my open hands. I rested my forehead to his.

Running my hands gently over his soft muzzle, I could tell he had gotten severely sandblasted staying off the pace. He looked like he had two black eyes, the lids were so puffy. When he opened them enough for me to see, I discovered the sand had pitted and peeled his normally bright brown eyes, leaving them marred, dull and hazy.

When Stanley kept pushing his head into my arms while blinking and rolling his eyes, it was apparent the damage caused by the sand was bothering him a great deal. Because the injury could easily turn into a dangerous infection, I retrieved an eye ointment the vet had given me for this type of situation. Stanley just laid his head over my shoulder as I flushed his eyes out with eyewash to rid them of any remaining grains of sand, and then applied the ointment. Those eyes really did look so painful. They would heal within the next few days, but during that time we went through a lot of ointment.

Stanley rewarded my ministrations after the Derby with a full-body head rub of such force that I had to lean into him to keep from being pushed over. When he settled, he stood there while I hugged him, my arms around his neck. I scratched his withers until I found just the right spot. He bobbed his head, cocked a hind foot and finally relaxed.

Jim and I spent several more hours at the barn, exhausted but not yet ready to leave our horse. As usual, Stanley was tickled to have the company. He was obviously tired but still quite chipper. We had to leave eventually so that he could rest, but still, as much as I had wanted this day to be over, I was now reluctant for it to end.

Just before I stepped into the car, I stopped and gazed at the twin spires. They were beautifully lit against the dark of the night, as before. I turned my head back to where the dark silhouette of my horse stood out starkly against the light from within his stall.

In that moment I paused to consider the Kentucky Derby again. It was no longer a dream to pursue—it had become part of my reality. We may not have won, but I still had my wonderful horse. Other than his eyes, he was healthy, and he had come out of the race mentally in great shape.

Casual Lies had been challenged when the mighty Arazi had tried to go by him on the final turn. As I had predicted, the little horse couldn't get past my much bigger horse that afternoon. Ultimately, Arazi finished eighth, more than seven lengths behind Casual Lies.

Once again lost in the moment, I realized the twin spires of Churchill Downs were not going to represent a missed opportunity for me. As I stood between the spires and my horse, I felt the historic grandstand and its crowning glory would hold my bit of history in trust for the next ambitious dreamer who gazed up with awe and wonder, as had I. Just maybe our participation and honorable finish would inspire not only other women, but every dreamer—no matter how humble their beginnings—to follow our example and dare to reach for the impossible.

Although our moment in history had come and gone, when I slipped into the car I didn't need to wait until Sunday to know every single minute of that seemingly endless day had been worth it. I released a deeply held sigh, smiling as I reached out and squeezed Jim's hand. For the first time in a long time I could relax and simply let tomorrow bring its promise of another good day for Stanley and the man and woman who so deeply appreciated his courage, his talent and the phenomenal experience he had given them.

Chapter Twelve
On to Pimlico

I woke up the next morning without a voice, literally. Gone...not a croak, nor even a whisper. Surprisingly, there wasn't any pain, but when I tried to speak I could feel my throat vibrate with absolutely no sound. This was not a great situation for a person who loves to talk as much as I do, and did I ever have a lot to say.

When Jim and I arrived at the barn, a chipper if slightly subdued Stanley awaited our arrival. He stood all by himself—no guard, no reporters, no other horses in the stalls around him. He seemed somehow vulnerable.

The lack of activity felt very strange after the frenetic atmosphere of the last two weeks. It felt like all the air had gone out of the party balloons. The single red rose in the white Styrofoam cup had disappeared from the rail in front of Stanley's stall. Somehow it seemed fitting that it was gone, just like our lead in the Kentucky Derby had been stolen by Lil E Tee.

While Stanley finished his breakfast, Jim and I decided to head over to the media center for a cup of coffee and a roll. As we rounded the last barn before the track came into view, we saw something literally so amazing that it took a few seconds for the brain to register and make sense of what the eye was seeing.

Soaking-wet garbage covered everything in sight. Media types and a few racing officials were gingerly tiptoeing their way through this instant landfill.

Everywhere we looked we saw remnants of hundreds of discarded picnics along with an amazing number of broken lawn chairs, crushed ice coolers and a variety of just things. It looked like a thousand garbage trucks had exploded, a tornado had struck and then the downpour from the evening before had soaked the pulverized debris.

I hadn't realized that an informal press party would take place at the media center the morning after the race or we wouldn't have walked up there for our coffee. I wasn't in any condition to be giving interviews of any type, and Jim didn't ever like doing them.

The reporters spotted us before we could turn back, the questions started flying. Unfortunately for the reporters my answers were totally grounded. When one brave soul stuck a microphone in my face, I couldn't help but laugh, albeit soundlessly, shoulders shaking. I kept pointing to my throat, but it didn't seem to matter to them. They were willing to try lip reading. I found the best I could do was nod for yes, shake for no and smile a lot.

A truly delighted band of reporters and media types had a lot of laughs at my expense that morning. I lived through more tired and stale jokes than I can ever remember about how people lose their voice. I shook my finger at their outrageousness time and again.

Then there was the story making the rounds about what had taken place in my box after yesterday's race. It was being reported I had fainted dead away in the box seats when Casual Lies had run second, and the tale was taking on a life of its own. Thus the most popular question being asked was if this story was true.

I was helpless to deny it without a voice. I tried writing down my denial on a napkin, but nobody wanted, nor was willing, to believe me. Therefore, it went down into Kentucky

Derby lore how Shelley Riley, overcome by the moment, fainted after victory was snatched away from her horse—Casual Lies—in the last few strides of the Kentucky Derby. When all was said and done, the reporters were just having fun with us, and I basked in the warmth of their camaraderie.

The second most popular question that needed to be answered that morning was whether or not we would be going on to Pimlico Racetrack and the Preakness Stakes in Maryland. We were certainly encouraged by Stanley's impressive performance, and so far he seemed to have pulled up well from the race. Added to that, we were already nominated to the Triple Crown and thus the Preakness Stakes. A big smile and a nod of the head provided the easy answer to the insistent inquiries everywhere we went.

Unfortunately, the trash dished up over the next few days wasn't just on the track. Some of the racing press felt the need to cover their behinds after their beloved and overwhelming favorite Arazi failed to finish in the money. Those handicappers who had picked and declared Arazi as unbeatable had some explaining to do.

The morning of the press conference, a few journalists pleasantly surprised me by, if not in print, taking a good-hearted verbal poke at themselves and their picking prowess. In fact, a rumor circulated that crow was about to make the endangered species list in Kentucky.

As the days went by, we heard plenty of pithy comments and thinly veiled witticisms about Arazi's failure to leave the Derby field in his dust. I was told Andy Beyer, who had written "Casual Lies simply wasn't good enough to win the Kentucky Derby," had defended his soundly defeated first choice by calling the Derby field a bunch of crows and had opined Arazi was obviously undertrained. That statement certainly gave me pause for thought. It seemed to me any crow who had escaped to that point would have been well advised to head for the hills and stay there until the Triple Crown races were over.

We had been introduced to Joe DeFrancis, the president of Pimlico, at the morning-after media party and were very impressed by his eagerness to help us with anything we might need when we reached Baltimore. Joe assured us that rice hulls would be waiting when Casual Lies arrived at Pimlico. What a relief that was going to be.

I didn't want to van a tired horse and take the chance of knocking him out. So I made arrangements to ship to Baltimore by air toward the end of the week. We liked it in Kentucky, and I felt it would be better for Stanley to rest in what were now familiar surroundings for him. With two weeks between races, we'd still have a full week to get accustomed to the Pimlico strip before the Preakness Stakes took place.

We found we were not alone in our assessment. Lil E. Tee and Dance Floor would be among those traveling on the plane with us when we headed out. So Jim and I kicked back, toured a few more farms and fielded numerous telephone calls from an excited press, all requesting interviews.

One of those calls came from Toni Slotkin, an associate director and producer for ABC Sports. Toni's job was to produce a feature for the network's *Up Close and Personal* segment to be aired during the Preakness broadcast. Now that we were considered a legitimate contender, not just an oddity, ABC Sports wanted to highlight what was fast becoming one of the biggest human interest stories of the Triple Crown.

Mail was pouring in from people all over the country and beyond. I found the ever-increasing number of fans truly amazing and felt complimented by way of the interest they showed. That alone was certainly incentive enough to cooperate fully with ABC Sports and Toni. The fans, in my opinion, deserved to enjoy the fantasy aspect of my improbable dream, right along with us.

The story about Casual Lies trained by Shelley Riley was quickly turning into a story about Shelley Riley, the trainer of Casual Lies. At some point, the focus had shifted, and the media train was gathering speed.

~

WE SPENT THE REST OF the week with Stanley, letting him graze in the sun while we relaxed, re-centering ourselves after the whirlwind we had just survived. It was a pleasant time that ended when the day came to get our team ready to fly to Baltimore. Since I had not accompanied Jim and Stanley on the initial flight to Kentucky, this was going to be a whole new experience.

Flying has never been one of my favorite forms of travel, and flying with horses promised to be harrowing, at least for me. However, we had no viable alternatives, and once all the horses taking the flight were loaded on two vans, we were off to the airport.

As the drivers pulled through security, a baggage cart was waiting with a large lettered sign attached that read: "Follow this Way." The horse vans toured the outskirts of the runways to a remote area, where the specially outfitted flying horse van awaited our arrival. Each truck pulled up in turn to the equine loading ramps, and in very short order we were all aboard and on our way.

Once again we had Stanley in a larger stall at the front of the plane, and I was worried at how his ears kept scraping the ceiling of the plane. He would put his head up and test his headroom but seemed remarkably calm about it all.

The flight crew invited me to sit in the cockpit, in a jump seat directly behind the pilot. I was given headphones so I could listen to the air traffic comments they routinely heard.

As we approached the airport in Baltimore and the pilot positioned the plane for landing, the descent seemed so much more dramatic from my cockpit jump seat. It was the most amazing sight to see the trees reaching up their limbs as if to caress the fuselage while we drifted closer and closer to the earth.

Looking out the windshield with a pilot's eye view, I felt that those trees were so close and big that we were going to tangle our wheels and be torn from the sky. I had to hold my breath to keep from backseat driving. As my fingernails dug into my jump seat, an explosive "watch out" was never far from my lips.

Despite the professional flight crew's success in landing safely, once back on the ground I was extremely pleased to be riding with 18 wheels on the road as the van negotiated the backstreets to Pimlico.

~

WHEN THE VANS PULLED UP to the loading dock at the end of the Preakness barn, a number of reporters and photographers were gathered awaiting our arrival. The clackety-clack of camera shutters punctuated the activity as questions were called out while each horse was carefully led down the ramp.

Thus it all began anew—fewer reporters but, alas, more interest. Although the worldwide press contingency had departed with Arazi's return to Europe, plenty of eager new U.S. newspaper reporters lobbed questions to satisfy their readers' increasing interest in the story of the unlikely woman trainer and her bargain-basement horse. Of course, my focus was getting Stanley tucked safely into his new stall in the stakes barn.

Being stabled in the historic Preakness barn at Pimlico was nearly as exciting as seeing the twin spires at Churchill Downs for the first time. At Churchill, you didn't know who might have once been stabled in the stall your horse was occupying. At Pimlico, such was not the case because the occupants of the first three stalls are, with few exceptions, a matter of history. The first stall is allocated to the winner of the Kentucky Derby, the second to the runner up and so on. I found it astonishing and very satisfying to stand there and see my wonderful horse looking back at me from the very same stall that had housed so many truly great horses. It brought home the fact that we had earned this honor, that we belonged and that it wasn't over yet.

I doubt, however, that any other horse in the entire history of the Preakness had ever been bedded on what my horse was now standing on—rice hulls!! Glory hallelujah!

~

WHEN WE LED STANLEY UP to the stall with "Casual Lies" printed on the header, we found whoever bedded the stall must have been unfamiliar with rice hulls. It was bedded so generously that we could barely get in the stall without a ramp. Once in, both Jim and Stanley bogged down. It had to be at least two feet deep in rice hulls—I couldn't reach the bottom. All I could do was go in and bank the sides of the stall with the rice hulls until Stanley could move around the center with ease.

Stanley was happy, we were happy and there were enough rice hulls in the stall alone to last two months, not to mention what was in the feed room.

When I cleaned Stanley's stall the next morning, I ran

across several shiny hard black beetles. They were about an inch long and half an inch around. They had long legs at the back with each set getting shorter as they neared the front, and they looked like they had wings, but in fact they did not.

In California we called them stinkbugs. When disturbed, they would use their long back legs to raise up their rear end and blast some offensive odor. I never saw these bugs do that, but they looked just like California stinkbugs. I would pick them up in a coffee cup and pitch them out into the shedrow.

To my amazement, they would scramble back to the stall door and storm right back in. They seemed to like rice hulls as much as we did. However, the bigger problem with these bugs had yet to surface.

I noticed Stanley yawning a lot the next morning and acting fidgety, shaking his head excessively for no apparent reason. Having gone through the allergic reaction problem with him at Churchill Downs, I was on the lookout for anything unusual. We kept a careful eye on him all day, and he seemed to get more relaxed as the day wore on, even lying down to take a nap. Since my antenna was up, I determined we would come out and check him again after dark.

Jim and I returned later in the evening, and rather than disturb the whole barn by turning on the overhead lights, I borrowed a flashlight from one of the guards on duty. When we turned the flashlight on in Stanley's stall, much to my horror, we found him standing in the middle of a moving carpet of black bugs. Apparently, hundreds of these nocturnal critters buried themselves several inches down along the edges of the stall, only coming out when it got dark.

Poor Stanley was trying to sleep with these hard-shelled, claw-footed critters scrambling all over him, scratching at his eyes and climbing in his ears and up his nose. No wonder he was tired in the morning.

We went in with the muck basket and spent hours sifting and scooping up hundreds of these creepy crawlers. We carried them out to the muck pile at the far end of the barn. I dumped them and figured it would take several weeks for them to safari all the way from the muck pile back to the stall.

I don't know if the bugs had come with the rice hulls or if they were permanent residents of Pimlico. I never heard anybody else complain about them, and we didn't have them once we got to Belmont Park. Every day I would search for pockets of bugs as I cleaned Stanley's stall, and I rarely saw more than a couple at a time after the initial onslaught.

~

SINCE WE WERE STABLED NEXT to Lil E Tee, the winner of the Kentucky Derby, we spent some time chatting with his trainer, Lynn Whiting. I found him to be an easygoing guy with a warm personality. He did take off with my rake on a regular basis, though. At least after the first day I knew where to go to look for it.

As I walked Stanley one morning, I met trainer Nick Zito around the corner at the other end of the barn and got to rub on Strike the Gold, the 1991 winner of the Kentucky Derby. Nick had entered him in the Pimlico Special, which would be contested the Saturday before the Preakness.

Nick was quite a character, with a huge personality. He could be quite mercurial but incredibly charming when he wanted to be. Along with his distinctive New York accent, Nick was very quick-witted, glib and funny, if somewhat sarcastic at times. I liked him instantly, perhaps mostly because he was so multi-dimensional and filled to bursting with self-confidence.

I told Nick that I felt there was no way Strike the Gold could get outrun. And he didn't. I watched the race grinning from ear to ear, totally thrilled for Nick and Strike the Gold as they notched another victory.

D. Wayne Lukas was also stabled at the other end of the shedrow with his Preakness entry, Dance Floor. The rapper M. C. Hammer owned Dance Floor, a very nice horse who had run against us in several races.

At that time there was something about Wayne that I found intimidating. He was too smooth, too confident, too something. It was kind of like creeping past the towering quarterback in high school, hopefully going unnoticed lest you garner his disdain.

One day I was creeping past Wayne's end of the barn, looking neither left nor right, hoping for anonymity. Suddenly, he stepped to the railing and halted me in my tracks with a casual greeting and an enormous smile. I was struck dumb. As I tried to regain my composure and unglue my feet from the pavement, Wayne carried on chatting as if I had responded to his greeting.

It took time, but I eventually became very comfortable with Wayne's complicated, cultivated and polished blend of sophisticated, down home, good ol' boy, college coach persona. He was also a fine horseman. I witnessed Wayne Lukas on his knees in a stall putting polo bandages on one of his charges. He did a good job too. What I can't figure out is how he kept so clean. He always looked like he'd been Simonized.

~

SINCE I WOULDN'T COMMIT TO racing at Pimlico completely until after we had seen how we finished in the Kentucky Derby, getting a hotel was not easy, at least not close in at that late a date. We were forced to venture farther out and ended up at the Marriott in Hunts Valley, about a 25-minute drive out off the beltway.

Thankfully, Chrysler provided us with yet another new car to use, only this time Pimlico assigned a driver to ferry us everywhere. A driver was a great addition and a very nice touch.

Bill Ritmiller was a lieutenant with the Baltimore City Police Department. He loved racing and took a vacation each year so he could drive for one of the Preakness participants. I would have felt like the character played by Whitney Houston if the movie *The Bodyguard* had been out earlier that year. However, Bill was considerably friendlier than Kevin Costner's character in the film.

What a great time we had with our newfound friend. He must have had the most patient wife in the world, because the extra travel time he had to put in before and after he picked us up kept him going a good 18 to 20 hours on some days.

Poor Bill was invariably dropping us off no earlier than 10 at night and even later on other nights due to all the scheduled events. He would return to pick us up right on the stroke of 5 a.m. the next morning. I would come out and find him waiting, sound asleep, behind the wheel of the car. If he hadn't had fresh clothes on, I would have thought he'd slept in the car overnight.

When we finished at the barn in the morning, I would get Bill to show us around Baltimore and even farther out in the countryside. We were, after all, simply tourists at heart, and he was a very accommodating tour guide. It was great because we wouldn't need to worry about getting lost in the red-light district or somewhere else equally dangerous. In fact, Bill laughed a lot when I asked him to give us a tour of the red-light district.

We were deluged with invitations. We went to press parties, Preakness parties and private parties. It was a glitter of famous faces, spectacular venues and paparazzi.

One night on our way to a party at the Aquarium, I jokingly asked Bill if he was packing. He laughed and shook his head in disbelief. I never did find out if he was armed or not. I tried to get him to open the trunk of the car to see if he hid his gun in there. He put the car keys in his pocket and walked off. I heard him chuckling at my audacity as I trailed along behind.

~

PIMLICO DIDN'T HAVE ONE OF the most beautiful barn areas I have ever seen. "Grim" would be the best description of what I first saw from the big rig we rode in on. I was reminded of the old pictures of Cannery Row in Monterey before it was restored and turned into a tourist attraction.

The Preakness barn, the last in a long row, was well maintained and very nice. We were stabled on the side that faced a grassy area running the full length of the barn. This area, separated from the shedrow by a wide swath of blacktop, was enclosed by a split-rail fence and had a row of eight-foot evergreens along the far fence to buffer us from the noise of the busy city street beyond. This layout effectively isolated us from the rest of the barn area, and we enjoyed a nice air of tranquility. The horses could take in the sun in the afternoon while grazing on this green oasis. It was also a great spot for on-air interviews.

I was finding it ever more entertaining to banter back and forth with all the quick-witted reporters who showed up and hung around the Preakness barn. They liked me because I made it easier for them to fill their columns. Whenever it got to be too much, I would either go into Stanley's stall or into the feed room to hide out for a while.

The barn itself was quite long, with a dirt shedrow and outside rail for hand-walking the horses. The downside was the narrowness of the shedrow, and with the number of horses walking nearly on top of us as they passed, it was quite difficult to get our chores accomplished in a timely manner each day.

One of the horses scheduled to run in the Preakness was named Conte Di Savoya. Trained by LeRoy Jolley, he had run fourth in the Kentucky Derby and had a rather unfortunate reputation that preceded him wherever he went.

A big horse with a nasty disposition, he was reputed to be a rogue and quite dangerous. On the Wednesday before the Preakness, after working a half-mile, Conte Di Savoya apparently savaged his lead pony and threw his jockey, Walter Guerra. The horse then went out of his way to intentionally kick Walter as he fell to the ground, breaking several of the rider's ribs.

Sometime later, as I was walking Stanley around the shedrow in a long line of other horses, I saw Conti reaching out from his stall, ears flattened back, nasty as a snake, threatening each passing horse and handler. On alert now, I thought I was ready for him and angled Stanley as far to the right side of the shedrow as possible. Since I was walking on Stanley's left, I was between him and Conti.

After the horse directly in front of me walked past Conti, I watched the rogue suck back and disappear into the depths of his stall. I thought for an instant that I might have gotten lucky, until I heard him thundering around. Just as Stanley and I came abreast of Conti's stall, I glanced to my left and saw a flash of movement.

Conti charged forward, slamming into the stall guard with all his weight, his momentum bowing it out. With rage-filled eyes, ears slicked back to his head, he opened his mouth as wide as he could get it, teeth bared. It was truly a frightening sight.

Instinctively I turned into Stanley, plastering myself to his side. Conti hit me so hard it felt like I had been hit with a baseball bat. Since I was trapped up against well over a thousand pounds of horse, there was no give. I took the full force of the blow right over my left kidney.

Fortunately Stanley maintained his manners and his cool as I leaned against him, fairly helpless. I laid one arm over his withers, and Stanley more or less carried me away from the savage behind us.

Once out of reach, Stanley stopped, and I found I was having trouble getting my breath. A nerve leading to my leg must have been temporally affected because I was dragging my foot. Jim rushed to my side, and everybody wanted to know if I was okay. I wasn't, but I certainly didn't want to cry in front of all the cameras. Jim took Stanley while I leaned over the rail trying to recover.

As I gasped for breath, I could see a crowd gathered around a guy with a television camera. He was replaying something for them on his screen. I heard plenty of gasps, ooh's and ahh's, along with a lot of high fiving. Having his camera trained on me for most of the morning, he had caught the whole attack on film.

Later, he added the theme music from "Jaws," and it hit the networks. It seemed to play forever on the sports blooper channels.

I had a swelling the size of a small football on my back, with jagged red and blue teeth marks bordering the bulge. I was urged to go to the hospital in case my kidney had been bruised. I felt that if there was no apparent blood, I couldn't be hurt that badly. Besides, Stanley needed me. So I limped around for a few days, hunched over like Quasimodo while the press went crazy over the attack.

We had captured a great deal of the attention that had previously been lavished on Arazi. For better or for worse, it seemed we were now the story du jour of the Triple Crown season.

Chapter Thirteen

Preakness Stakes, the Second Jewel

Who would have thought Shaquille O'Neal, one of the three most sought-after choices for the National Basketball Association's 1992 draft, could affect the outcome of that year's draw for the Preakness Stakes? Certainly not me—I had never even heard of him. My mom, on the other hand, was a North Carolina native who watched college basketball with an unholy glee. Her favorite was North Carolina State University, with Duke University a close second in her affections.

As Jim and I trooped over to Pimlico's Sports Palace the morning of the Preakness draw, we were discussing the condition of the track and how we hoped the sun would either emerge to dry out the surface or that it would just go ahead and pour down rain. A muddy track would be a blessing compared to the hard yet slippery condition caused by the gentle, steady rain currently underway.

When we galloped Stanley later, we found the surface was, crudely put, as slick as snot on a glass doorknob. Stanley had bobbled and slipped every step of the way, and Jim was sure he would injure himself before he could get him off the greasy surface. It was obvious that he wasn't going to handle the track if it stayed in its present condition come Preakness day.

Once we arrived at the Sports Palace, we found the post-position draw was going to be televised. The place was filled, with quite a party atmosphere already in place. Pimlico had arranged for Wes Unseld, a former NBA player and then head coach of the Washington Bullets, to pull the entries for post positions.

When everybody finally settled down and the draw was set to begin, I was fidgeting and anxious as usual. The luck of the draw was going to play just as big a part in the Preakness as it had in the Kentucky Derby. Fourteen horses would be going to post, a lot of horses for Pimlico's narrow track and notoriously tight turns.

Quiet settled over the Sports Palace, and the players for the draw were all in position. Unseld pulled the first entry out of the box as a numbered pill was rolled out of the leather bottle. For better or worse, that entry form and that pill were a mated pair, and nothing could change the horse's post position now that the draw was done.

Unseld looked down at the horse named on the entry form, and then he looked up at the anxiously waiting crowd, paused for dramatic effect and called out in an excited baritone, "Shaquille O'Neal."

After a long moment of silence, an explosion of male laughter filled the room. I had no idea what was so funny until Jim informed me the NBA draft was coming up and Shaquille O'Neal was expected to be the first player chosen in the first round of the draft.

Unseld then stuck the entry back in the box, and the pill went back into the bottle. I was stunned.

"Oh my god, did you see that?" I gasped.

"What?" Jim said.

"He just put the entry back in the box. The whole luck of the draw just went up in smoke."

As we waited, I squirmed in discomfort and felt sick to

my stomach. When Casual Lies was called with post position eight, I felt relieved. That was a great post for us. However, M.C. Hammer's horse, Dance Floor, a horse I greatly respected, came out of the draw on the extreme outside in post 14. It was the worst post position possible, especially for a horse who liked to run from just off the pace.

Although I could understand Unseld's playing to the media in a lighthearted moment, apparently no one had explained the importance of the draw to him beforehand or else he probably wouldn't have done what he did. The draw is supposed to be inviolable in its integrity at any level of racing, let alone a once-in-a-lifetime opportunity like the Preakness.

I certainly wasn't going to say anything. My horse got the number eight post, which was terrific. The last thing I would have wanted to see was the race re-drawn, which would not have restored the integrity that had already been compromised.

The rumor started circulating rather quickly that the M.C. Hammer camp was furious with the official results of the draw. People were talking about it up and down the shedrow. Apparently, they were quite vocal, finding it rather suspicious that Dance Floor had gotten the worst post possible in the Preakness after he had drawn even farther out in the Kentucky Derby.

The rumor mill also had Hammer storming away from his trainer, D. Wayne Lukas, threatening to scratch his horse. I know if it had been me, I would have felt snake bit. To my knowledge the irregularity in the draw that morning has never been mentioned by anyone, in print or otherwise.

My little posse kept its own council. What was the point of starting up a controversy when there was no fair remedy to be had? Over the years I have always wondered what horse's name was on that entry form and what number was on that pill. For all I know, it could have been Casual Lies and the number 14.

~

EVERY MORNING THE CROWD of reporters grew, and I finally had to make it clear that my work with Casual Lies must come first. I would exchange one-liners in passing, but if they wanted my undivided attention, they would have to wait until I had time.

As we were taking a short break in the feed room one morning, I looked up to see someone peering in the door with a camera cocked and ready. He quickly snapped a picture of me with a great big donut in my hand and hastily departed. "Charming, that'll look lovely," I said to myself.

Even though the media captured our every move and relayed our every word, we were still off to the track with Casual Lies for each of his morning jaunts as usual. What was bizarre, and something I would never get used to, was the herd of journalists and television cameramen running ahead of us to set up for a good shot. Déjà vu—it certainly harkened back to what Arazi had endured before the Kentucky Derby at Churchill Downs, albeit this was on a much smaller scale. Stanley, unlike Arazi, took it all in stride. He liked the attention, and he loved the leisurely stroll under the trees that lined the bridle path leading to the track at Pimlico.

~

WALKING THE TRACK THE morning of the Preakness, we were hopeful that the track condition would have improved; instead we found things hadn't changed for the better or worse. The weather, while not foul, was less than delightful.

Overcast with a light mist that kept the air thick with moisture, it would have made a perfect environment if you were an orchid. The track still had about two inches of slick wet dirt over a hard-packed base.

I felt gutted and wasn't looking forward to letting so many people down if Stanley weren't able to handle the slippery surface. But I could still hope for the track to dry out over the long day ahead.

When our chauffeur, Bill, had dropped us off the night before, he encouraged us to be ready to spend the entire day at the track because a huge turnout of racing fans would likely cause a traffic gridlock. What I'd seen on the streets as we drove to the track that morning had intrigued me. Not dissimilar to Louisville and yet with its own style, entrepreneurship was alive and well. Barbeques were smoking away in any number of front yards wherever cars weren't being parked for a fee. But the really entertaining sight was the gang members, flying their colors and, for a small charge, pushing shopping carts filled with a family's picnic baskets from the family's car to the grandstand gates.

People from ABC came by and asked me to please reconsider wearing a sound pack for this race. I agreed, but as we started the long walk over to the grandstand, I was already regretting it. The transmitter must have weighed a pound, and it was supposed to be hooked to my waistband, with an ear bud running up to my ear so I could answer questions on air. Though it was not overly noticeable, I had lost a bit of weight since I had bought the outfit. It was pretty baggy, and the slacks kept threatening to come down with the weight of the sound pack.

Here we were being followed by any number of camera crews, tiptoeing through the muck on the track, and I was holding my pants up with both hands. We crossed the main track near the head of the lane and walked down the turf course. A staging area had been set up on that turf course directly in front of the grandstand. It was lovely, with space for each horse designated by a hand-painted Black-eyed Susan on a tall stand. All the colors contrasted beautifully with the green of the turf as glamorous people mingled with the trainers, jockeys and gorgeous horses.

With such a wide open space surrounding us, it was difficult getting Stanley to stand still long enough to do anything with him. He was definitely on the muscle and looking for trouble. To Stanley, the large span of unobstructed space presented an opportunity to stampede around and display his deeply ingrained desire to play and show off. There was no doubt he would kick somebody if they got close enough.

Jim was leading Stanley around in a tight circle, trying to keep him out of the range of other horses as well as the VIPs who were wandering blithely all over the place. They seemed blissfully unaware that they weren't above getting a painful kick.

I heard Jim bark at someone, "Get back, you're going to get kicked."

I'd been busy watching out for myself as I endeavored to respond intelligently to everyone who was trying to talk to me, including the voice in my ear bud. But after the third time Jim snarled, "I'm telling you, you are going to get kicked," I looked around.

Standing right behind me was Oprah Winfrey with a large group of people. Startled by the tone of Jim's warning, I said to him, "Don't snarl at Oprah." He just looked disgusted as he struggled to keep Stanley under control.

Oprah looked star-struck while she gazed at Stanley and shook my hand.

"I wanted to see Stanley, both of them," she said. The other Stanley Oprah was referring to was her friend, M.C. Hammer, whose actual name was Stanley Burrell. Flashing her engaging smile, she said in her oh-so-mellow Oprah voice, "I have two Stanleys to root for. I don't know which one I want to win more."

Thank goodness for all the photographers because I have several pictures of Oprah Winfrey hugging me.

Then it was riders up, and when the first horse stepped onto the main track, the band started up with "Maryland, My Maryland." This time I got to see and hear my horse parade, and it was truly awesome. So many years I had watched the Preakness on television, and now I was a part of the big event.

We made our way to our box with a contingent of large television cameras in tow. I found it a little embarrassing to have so many cameras waiting to catch every nuance of the emotions I was feeling. The people surrounding us were spending more time staring at me than at the horses parading to the gate. Knowing that everything I said could be played back at a later date, I felt like I needed a muzzle stuffed with cotton to prevent me saying anything embarrassing.

A roar went up when Casual Lies' name was announced during the loading of the horses in the starting gate. What a high—and it just goes to show the power of the media. The coverage had even included a whole page of the *Washington Post* "Style" section dedicated to telling the story of Casual Lies and Shelley Riley. No racehorse had ever before been featured in the Style section of the *Washington Post*. The crowd's thunderous response to my colt's name at the starting gate made it clear that our story had touched many people, and that somewhere along the way Stanley had become as real to them as he was to me.

The cheering of more than 90,000 fans made a fast fade when the last of the horses were loaded. The gate opened, and the whole field broke cleanly. Casual Lies seemed in good position as they ran down the lane for the first time. Around the first turn, he maintained a position between fourth and fifth place while the early speed dug in on the front end. Between the half-mile and the three-eighths poles on the backstretch, however, Casual Lies started dropping back alarmingly. I couldn't keep track of him, and I couldn't hear the race caller above the crowd.

With the exception of the front-runners, the horses were so coated with mud that they all began to look the same. I knew Casual Lies wasn't in front and he wasn't last, but I had no idea where he was in between those two extremes.

Then Jim yelled, "Here he comes!"

I looked for him frantically, my eyes scanning from front to back of the surging, mud-covered field of horses. I still couldn't distinguish Casual Lies from the pack, but I saw a horse making a huge bid halfway around the turn. My gaze latched onto that horse as he made a very impressive move three wide, gaining ground with every stride.

Just as I recognized that the horse was indeed Casual Lies, I saw Gary Stevens make a great move of his own, angling Stanley to the inside, where there was room left to run down the stretch. That's not always a good idea on a wet track because quite often the rail is where the going's the heaviest, but in this instance it was the only choice—and proved to be the right one.

Casual Lies was catching horses rapidly, but we were running out of real estate faster than we were running out of horses to pass. The finish wire came before Casual Lies could catch Pine Bluff, who won, and Alydeed, who finished second. Stanley ended up third, in front of the unlucky Dance Floor, who had made his bid and then weakened going down the lane.

Less concerned with our finish in the race than I was with the health of my horse, Jim and I hurried down to check on Stanley and hear what Gary Stevens had to say after the horses returned to be unsaddled.

After Gary pulled the mud-encrusted tack off Stanley, he voiced his amazement at how game Casual Lies had been during the race. He explained that the footing on the track was so slick that Stanley was stumbling and sliding as if he would go down at any moment. He also mentioned that Stanley had spit out the bit on the backstretch, at which point the field quickly pulled away from him. Having given up all hope for a finish in the top three, Gary said he then focused on keeping my horse safe and out of trouble for the remainder of the race.

I watched Gary's mud-covered face break into a smile. He shook his head and said in wonder, "Then all of sudden, halfway around the turn, he picked the bit back up and started running, passing horses even though he was still floundering all over the place." Gary's comments helped reassure both Jim and me that our horse was fine and that his gritty nature had prevailed over the miserable racing surface and was still intact.

After big races like those in the Triple Crown, when the horse is unsaddled, the valet peels off the saddlecloth and it goes back to the barn with the horse. Generally, these saddlecloths have the name of the horse and his post number stitched, embroidered or glued on. They make great souvenirs, and some of them can become quite valuable to collectors. The Preakness towel, with its bright yellow and black coloring, was so sandblasted that the letters in Casual

Lies' name were peeling away from the cloth. I later learned that this condition made it even more valuable. In short, you never want to wash a saddlecloth after a race of this caliber.

It's hard to imagine how painful the beating for both rider and horse must be when the track is muddy. They are traveling so fast while enduring a continuous wall of mud clods pummeling them in the face and body. Jim used to come back after a race on a muddy track bruised over a wide area of his body. He said he had been hit by flying horseshoes that had torn off the horses' feet by the mud.

So Stanley's eyes would need more eye ointment, and though we were disappointed that we didn't win, we couldn't be disappointed in our horse. Stanley had shown a remarkable amount of grit on a slick surface that hadn't complemented his style of running in any way whatsoever.

It didn't take long for someone to tell me that our third-place finish was the best in the 117 runnings of the Preakness for a horse trained by a woman. Ten years later, I gave a tip of the hat to Nancy Albert and her Magic Weisner, who ran second in the 2002 Preakness.

~

WITH KENTUCKY DERBY winner Lil E. Tee failing to win the Preakness, there would be no Triple Crown champion for another year and no chance for that $5 million bonus. However, with our third, we had gained more points toward the million-dollar Triple Crown bonus that would be paid to the horse who acquired the most points while competing in all three races.

We would have to commit to run in the Belmont Stakes to qualify for a chance at winning that million-dollar carrot. Pine Bluff, the winner of the Preakness, was the only other horse who also had a chance at the bonus. That gave us a 50-

50 chance of leaving New York with a million dollars. There was no question that we would be heading for Belmont Park and the Belmont Stakes.

But not right away. I decided to delay our departure for New York so that Stanley could relax and recuperate in the quiet of the now-abandoned Preakness barn. This was quality time that Jim and I greatly appreciated, helping to settle our nerves, while we enjoyed our charming horse.

~

MORE FAN MAIL FOUND its way to us, and one of the joys of my day was reading those letters. One in particular grabbed my attention and moved me, not only then, but even now as I read through it once again.

Joanne LaRocco, a 16-year-old girl, had traveled by herself on a bus from New Jersey to see Casual Lies run in the Preakness. She wrote the following:

Dear Shelley,

I am 16 years old and love Casual Lies. I had the opportunity to go to the Preakness. Casual Lies is so beautiful. Casual Lies reached in and called upon his champion heart. He has a heart the size of his body. I admire the faith you have in Casual Lies. I too will never lose faith in your champion.

You made a terrific decision to keep Casual Lies. Selling him would be like selling your dream. He is a horse I dream of training someday. I wish to train just like you. Hope for the best and accept the rest. I will follow my dreams, just like you, and maybe I will be sending a "Casual Lies" to the Derby. Whether I do or not, I would be proud just to be involved in this exciting sport.

After each race at the Preakness, I would run from the

crowded grandstand area and up to the box seat entrance in hopes that you would enter or exit. I even missed part of the post parade. I was waiting for you. I would like to have shaken your hand and met the master trainer that you are. Unfortunately, the day ran out of races and I was on my way on the bus. I promised myself someday I'll meet my role model. And just someday I may.

I have a 16-year-old Quarter Horse named Skip. He is like my best friend. He never complains or yells at me. He just enjoys our time together. Behind my house are trails and fields. Every day we explore them together. I love to gallop him in the big fields. I sometimes imagine he is a Thoroughbred with the imperialism Casual Lies has and I am his trainer. I'm just breezing my "racehorse" and enjoying the beauty and good of the racing world. I dream someday I'll be on the track galloping my own Thoroughbreds and being proud of what they do for me and racing fans.

After I'm done galloping Skip, I take him in our old one-horse stall barn and treat him as if he was a racehorse stepping off the track. I give him liniment baths and everything else. Enclosed is a photo of my best friend, Skip.

I hope your back is feeling much better now. That was a shame. I hope Conte de Savoya learned some manners. He was just jealous of Casual Lies.

I do hope to meet you someday. We will be great friends seated in the box seats, watching our horses go to the post in the Kentucky Derby one day. We will be smiling, knowing our runners are giving all the courage their hearts carry.

If you ever want to talk about racing, please feel free to call me.

Love, Joanne LaRocco

If I had ever doubted the wisdom of opening up to the press and sharing my adventure with the public, this letter alone erased any and all of those doubts. To have such a lovely letter sent to me filled with the joy, faith and promise of youth was truly a tonic to the soul. To have such a wonderful young girl express herself so eloquently touched me on so many levels. I have never forgotten her and wish I could have met her.

As the week came to a close, we were the only occupant left in the Preakness barn. It was so peaceful that I sighed with submission when I arranged for a van to carry Casual Lies and us to New York. It turned out to be a 16-horse van, and my horse was the only one scheduled for pickup. Jim and I had a blast riding in the back with Stanley while running up and down like a couple of kids to take in the scenery out of both sides of the van as it traveled the highway to our destination.

During the trip, I had the opportunity to contemplate everything we had experienced so far and the opportunities that lay ahead for my team. Stanley was chipper and tapped a tattoo on the floor mats if we spent too much time looking out the windows instead of paying attention to him. My mind was never far from thoughts of him, however, and that was just the way Casual Lies liked it.

The Belmont Stakes—at the distance of a mile and half, the final jewel of the Triple Crown seemed as big as the huge city of New York itself and was scheduled only three weeks after the strenuous race we had just run. I scratched an eager Stanley behind his ears and promised him a big apple if he could conquer the one on our horizon.

I started singing the song "New York, New York" to Stanley, trying to get him to relax. Listening to the song's words, I came to realize how apropos the lyrics were for our circumstances. And thus the miles ticked off beneath the wheels of the big rig as we headed toward the finale in our three-act play.

Chapter Fourteen

The Big Apple

The Big Apple! I'm sure Casual Lies would have preferred the big carrot, but for the rest of the team, the former was just fine. The New York City celebrated in song, film and print was for us big, brash, noisy, chaotic, crowded, intimidating and decidedly wonderful.

As we rode into town in the back of a horse van, circumventing the center city turmoil, our first sights of New York City exceeded our expectations. But first there was Belmont Park, located in Elmont on Long Island, where we were anxious to get Stanley settled into his new abode.

Leonard Hale, the senior vice president of racing for the New York Racing Association, had come by our barn after the Preakness and invited us to Belmont Park. Lenny trucked Stanley's rice hulls from Pimlico to Belmont Park himself and handpicked the barn where we would be stabled. Not a single day passed during our entire stay in New York without a visit from this amazing ambassador for racing.

The barn that Lenny chose for us was a very special barn, historic in fact. Five consecutive Belmont stakes winners walked out of Barn 3, all trained by Hall of Famer Woody Stephens. I was thrilled to pieces to be the only Belmont Stakes contender asked to be stabled in his barn that year.

I'd never met Woody, but I soon learned he liked to reminisce—and I wasn't averse to listening. Woody Stephens,

Charlie Whittingham, Ron McAnally and Wayne Lukas—what a star studded cast of characters had come into my life and such vast depths of racing experience made available to me in a matter of weeks. Well, truth be told, when Wayne Lukas would pass by my barn, it wasn't to offer up advice. It was usually to ask if I had made the coffee yet. Cheeky bugger!

Stanley was still a little quiet and recovering from another set of very painful eyes. Although he didn't care what barn he was in as long as Jim and I were there to entertain him, the large grassy area between the barns—only steps from his stall—was his personal bliss.

He grazed in the sun, shaded by the huge trees, as a merry band of obstreperous Belmont squirrels chewed us out from on high. Stanley liked the squirrels. He would observe their antics, which held a fascination for him that I didn't quite understand. At least it wasn't a chicken or a goat.

~

WE CHOSE TO STAY CLOSE to Casual Lies, and to that end we checked into the Floral Park Motor Lodge on the Jericho Turnpike, five minutes from the track. The staff was delighted that we were staying with them rather than the fancy up-market hotel where the majority of the Belmont participants were ensconced. That hotel was over a half-hour's drive away, and I just couldn't deal with commuting again.

Since the phone never ceased its ringing, even late into the night, I would call the front desk and let them know we were taking a time out and the ringing would stop. From that point forward, they took a boatload of messages—not just the name and number, but the purpose for the call. It was like having my own private secretary.

215

While I shuffled through these messages, I found that Toni Slotkin and her crew from ABC Sports had been assigned to do another feature for the Belmont Stakes telecast. I also found a callback number for CBS, which turned out to be the producer for *On the Road with Charles Kuralt*, a weekly television series. Then one afternoon in the middle of a shower, I got a call from *Sports Illustrated*.

It was obvious that Casual Lies was not the big horse story of that year's Triple Crown. It was the story behind the horse that kept gaining momentum. To that end, *Sports Illustrated* wanted a bite out of the pie.

The magazine sent Douglas S. Looney, a freelance journalist, to spend an entire week with us. He followed us from the time we arrived at the barn in the morning until we were done in the afternoon. I knew I wasn't going to be featured on the cover in a swimsuit, but who would have thought I would have garnered more than a footnote on one of the back pages of *Sports Illustrated*? I got the centerfold.

After our amazing time with *Sports Illustrated*, we were off to New York with Toni and ABC. As we drove across the bridge into the city proper, I was struck nearly speechless by the sheer mass and pulsing energy of the city that is rumored to never sleep.

Toni and her crew took us to some of the typical tourist stops and many not so typical. I was told it's easy to tell the tourist in New York City from the natives. The natives never look up for fear of looking like a tourist and getting mugged.

I noticed a real style to driving in New York. The right hand stays on the wheel as close to the horn as possible, if not actively engaging it, something that occurs frequently. The left hand and arm are out the window giving hand signals if it's not raining, in which case the left hand takes over horn-honking duty.

The taxi drivers in particular also seemed to ascribe to the "don't look up" theory while working all four appendages simultaneously. The lines in the road appeared to be nothing more than a polite suggestion. I have never heard so much horn honking. I'm a Californian—if a horn honks, it's time to duck.

Toni took us to meet the boldest of them all, real New York construction workers at a Bendel Construction project in midtown. The guys were all hooting and whistling as we approached the site with Toni and her film crew. You would have thought they'd spotted a supermodel in hot pants instead of little ole me. I laughed and tried to show them some ankle. Fortunately for them, I was wearing slacks.

All work ceased at our approach as the large and burley crew greeted us. The boss was there to present me with a shiny new hardhat, and they treated me like the mayor of the city at a ribbon cutting when we toured the project. Gutting a pre-existing building and reconstructing it while the heartbeat of the city heaves and pulses along its periphery showed us what a logistical nightmare really is.

We chased street vendors down Fifth Avenue, literally. Only in New York City, two strings of pearls for $2! Real gold watches for $20? You just have to be able to run faster than the vendors to be able to buy anything. I think they could have been free agents for the NFL the way they ducked and dove through the pedestrian traffic.

Apparently, all the vendors were a bit camera-shy. If we'd wanted the real bargains they claimed could be had, ABC's camera crew needed to stay at home. It definitely takes less energy to shop the street vendors in San Francisco.

I had mentioned to Toni how I had always wanted a fur coat, so, of course, one of the stops was at a furrier, B. Smith & Sons. We were shown into their by-appointment-only showroom. I know I live in California, and I knew fur coats were the object of rabid activist protesters. But, oh my, they were lovely. I told Jim I could turn the air conditioner on high while running through the house in my full-length mink coat.

One thorough reality check later, along with a good deal of very sound reasoning, we left without the mink. I didn't leave New York empty-handed, however. I found an outrageously expensive imported Italian silk tie for Jim to wear with his suit on Belmont Stakes Day.

Toni was tickled to arrange a carriage ride through Central Park for me and Woody Stephens. Even seasoned New Yorkers had to stop and take a look as we rode through the park in the horse-drawn conveyance, a camera crew wedged in beside the coachman.

Walking along one of the avenues later on, I stopped at a vast flower stall. As I was filmed bent over sniffing a lovely bucket full of red roses, a passerby stopped and said to me, "Aren't you that woman? The one with the horse?" I straightened up, flashed the biggest smile I owned, and the man gushed about how he and his family loved watching Stanley and me on TV. He wished us good luck in the Belmont.

The camera crew was absolutely astounded. Not only had the man recognized me, but he'd taken the time to stop and share his enthusiasm. The crew related how they had been filming a major star outside a New York restaurant and very few people bothered to even turn their heads, let alone stop. I was definitely amused when they decided I was just more approachable, like a horse-crazy version of Barbara Bush.

We had dinner at the famous 21 Club. The manager was delighted to take us through the kitchen and gave us a personal tour of the wine cellar. The cellar had been used as a speakeasy during Prohibition, and it was fascinating to see the ingenious methods they had employed to try and foil detection by the Feds. Although the restaurant was raided countless times, the wine cellar with its speakeasy was never discovered. As we left, I gazed at the iron jockeys lining the staircase and envisioned the colors of my silks on one of those famous icons.

~

BURNING THE CANDLE AT both ends seemed to have become a way of life. But I intended to wring every available drop out of the experience. When Lynn Swann flew into New York and came by to visit us, I told him I couldn't help but feel a little sad that "this too shall pass."

Lynn relayed a bit of wisdom he was pretty sure originated with a Roman general riding in his chariot back to Rome: "Fame is fleeting, money is like grains of sand in your hand and character lasts forever." Proof positive that Lynn is not only a very witty guy and a lot of fun, but astute as well.

When anyone asked me if I would miss the attention after our return to California, Lynn's humorous bit of wisdom took on a whole new meaning. While on the one hand some quiet time had a great deal of appeal, on the other I recognized all good things come to an end and we would have plenty of quiet time soon enough. In the meantime, look out, New York. We had arrived, and we still had so much more to see, along with a host of memories to mint.

When the Charles Kuralt crew showed up at the barn after we had finished the morning chores, we were ready for another new adventure.

On the way in to the city, the producer Lei Ling shared Kuralt's vision with us and described the premise of the *On the Road* segments. Basically he wanted interesting short documentaries structured to show the American public heartwarming vignettes of ordinary people faced with extraordinary events.

We were going to be shown around New York and filmed as we enjoyed various venues in the exciting city for the first time. Then they would film us at the racetrack to capture, as they put it, "one day in the extraordinary life of an unlikely small-town woman trainer, and how she found herself competing at the highest level of a tough, male-dominated sport."

First stop, the Empire State Building. Having made prior arrangements, security hustled us past a long line of tourists waiting to take the elevator to the observation deck at the very top of the building. At various intervals along the roped-off queue, we breezed past signs designating the expected wait time. These signs were in hours, not minutes. I definitely felt guilty and conspicuous as we jumped the queue, sailing right along, camera crew in tow.

Crammed in the elevator with several curious occupants, I was asked for an autograph. It was flattering, but still, I felt like the most unlikely media star.

At the top of the Empire State Building, Jim and I had our picture taken with King Kong. Granted, he was rubber, three inches tall and dangled from a string attached to our fingers. Nevertheless, we were grinning from ear to ear. Peering over the edge at the vast city beyond, I quipped, "Look, Jim, there's the Daily Planet." Superman fans, we laughed together as our eyes scanned the skyline.

Fifth Avenue, St. Patrick's Cathedral, Gallagher's Steak House, Broadway—I glanced at Jim during the musical *Guys & Dolls* while we sat in the fifth row center with Toni, a tingle running along the back of my neck as the lyrics of the horseplayers' song "Fugue For Tinhorns" washed over me.

Change the horse's name in the song to Casual Lies and keep your fingers crossed. It felt like another omen to me.

Lenny arranged for Jim and me to have dinner in the city and enjoy the Broadway production of *Phantom of the Opera*. A huge black stretch limo picked us up at the Floral Park Motor lodge, blocking nearly the entire parking lot. When Jim and I left the theatre hours later, our chauffeur was waiting right out front and holding the door of the limo for us. We truly were living the life, at least for a while.

I had been looking forward to seeing the lights of New York reflected on the East River as we headed back to Elmont that night. However, in the city that never sleeps, here were two very happy but very tired tourists tucked away in the back seat of the limo, fast asleep. I am sure the lights twinkling fiercely on the shiny black surface of the river must have been beautiful, and although there would be other lights on other nights in time, I regret missing a memory of Manhattan's lights on the water that night with Jim.

~

DESPITE ALL THE HYPE and hoopla that surrounded me, threatening to distract me from my primary goal on a daily basis, one constant remained and served to bring Jim and me back to reality every morning. That was Stanley's brilliant gaze and energized greeting whenever we walked into the shedrow.

Stanley continued to recover quickly from the Preakness as the days went by, and he became more enthusiastic about his training. The first time we stepped onto the famous Belmont surface, the vastness of the track astounded us. I had never seen a track that was more impressive on scale alone. The majority of racetracks are one-mile ovals, but Belmont was half again as big with wide, sweeping turns.

From where I stood on the clubhouse turn without binoculars, Stanley represented little more than a speck of pepper to my eye as he galloped down the backstretch and into the distance. Anxious to hear what Jim thought about how Stanley had handled the surface, I started quizzing him almost before they left the track. Good news—Jim liked the track, and so did Stanley.

As the day approached to run for a million dollars, I couldn't help but ponder the possibilities. What would we do with a million dollars? I asked myself this question more frequently as Stanley continued to thrive with each day's passing.

One thing was for sure. I knew I wanted to have the opportunity to find out. At the same time, I tried not to dwell on the bonus or give it a lot of consideration until after it was earned. My main goal, after all, was to try to get my horse ready to win the Belmont Stakes. The million dollars and our place in history would take care of themselves.

The condition of the racetrack became more of a concern as race day approached. Rain had been pouring down for several days, threatening once again to affect the outcome of the race. Every track handles moisture differently, and we would have to run on it as it came up. There was one certainty—no matter what condition the track was in for the Belmont Stakes, Casual Lies would give nothing less than his best.

Fortunately, Gary Stevens felt the same way. As *Los Angeles Times*' racing reporter Bill Christine quoted him after the Preakness: "He ran third on guts alone. He didn't seem to be handling the track at all. He'd pick up the bridle for a few strides, then drop it. It was a gutty performance. . . . But I'm not disappointed, and the Belmont distance won't be a problem. My horse will gallop all day long. I don't think he liked the way the dirt was hitting him in the face in the Preakness."

I continued to receive ever-increasing numbers of fan mail, and one day an impressive-looking envelope arrived, having been forwarded to me from home. It was a personal letter from a Saudi prince and read as follows:

May 11, 1992

Dear Mrs. Riley,

When I bought Lear Fan as a yearling in 1982, I had a premonition that he would do well. Many other horses were bought and sold but never with the same conviction.

When he first stood at Gainesway Farm and I visited him, the same vibes came across, notwithstanding the decline in the equine industry as a whole and the prophets of doom decrying his potential.

Since I retained a majority shareholding in the syndicate, I have followed the progress of his progeny with a keen interest, albeit remotely. The story of Casual Lies has been quoted as a fairy tale, Cinderella reborn, etc. I did not share that view. I felt history was about to repeat itself since he appeared to be a chip off the old block. I happened to be in the U.S. on one of my too infrequent visits this year, and I watched the Kentucky Derby with a positive attitude.

Permit me to congratulate you on your success with him so far and wish you even more for the rest of the season. By copy of this letter I am asking Pat Payne, the Sales Director at Gainesway Farm, to give Lear Fan an extra carrot, two more sugar lumps and a pat on the shoulder for a job well done.

I am uncertain whether I shall still be in the U.S. on May 16th, but wherever fate happens to take me, I promise you my voice will be nearly as hoarse (!) as yours at the

Preakness.
Every best wishes,
H.R.H. Prince Ahmed Bin Salman Bin Abdulaziz

Now that was a surprise, and I had to smile when he mentioned the premonition and conviction he'd experienced with Lear Fan—the very same feelings I'd had with Casual Lies!—and the "prophets" who'd decried Lear Fan's chances just as they had Stanley's. This letter proved to me that these princes, with all their money and access to the very finest of everything, truly admired their horses. An extra carrot? Two more sugar lumps and a pat on the shoulder? Perhaps we weren't that different on at least one level. We both had a deep appreciation of the equine heart and loved to feed the spirit.

~

MORE PARTIES, MORE INTERVIEWS, television, radio and finally entry day arrived and the draw for post positions. Eleven horses were entered, a large field for the Belmont. We drew post position two, and I couldn't have been more delighted.

After missing the Kentucky Derby and skipping the Preakness, A.P. Indy had been deemed sound enough to run. He won the Peter Pan Stakes before being entered into the Belmont Stakes, and he drew post position one, inside of us and down on the rail.

Owner Robert Perez entered two horses in the race—Robert's Hero and the speedy Agincourt—and under the rules at the time, they were assigned wagering numbers 1 and 1A and were a single betting interest. The post positions did not correlate with the wagering numbers that appeared on the horses' saddlecloths, and Casual Lies, in post 2, would be wearing the wagering number 3.

Having run against A.P. Indy when he'd won both the

Hollywood Futurity and the Santa Anita Derby, I had studied the colt's running style for obvious reasons. It had been my observation that he didn't like to run up into an opening between a horse and the inside rail. He would run between horses and around horses, but if he was stuck down on the rail, his rider would bide his time until he could move him to the outside.

When racing a mile and a half, it isn't about post position as much as it is about strategy, unless, of course, you had much the best horse. But as far as I knew, none of the horses were going to run like Secretariat, who'd won the Belmont Stakes by a quarter of a mile.

The obvious speed was going to be Agincourt, but if he ran to form, he would peter out after a mile. Jim and I handicapped the race and felt the best strategy would be to get about three-quarters of length up on A.P. Indy while forcing him to stay down on the rail. Let the speed unfold on the front end, and we would stalk Pine Bluff, our only competition for the $1 million guaranteed payday. Winning the race would be the best possible of all outcomes, but to go home with a million-dollar bonus would be solace enough if we didn't cross the finish line first.

The day before the Belmont, somebody threw us a "Win the Belmont Party" under the trees next to our barn. There was plenty of food, drink and cake for the horsemen, television camera crews and reporters. Everybody there was high on possibilities, while I just wanted to win the race and put to rest the opinion, once and for all, that Casual Lies wasn't good enough to win a Grade I race.

CBS taped another interview, and then it was time to cut the cake. It was a large sheet cake with a depiction of Casual Lies posing on the front. Under the lenses of the cameras, I picked up the knife and made a straight cut right through his legs. When I looked down to make the second cut, I realized what I had just done. I felt sick. My superstitious side raised its ugly head, and I wanted so badly to rub out the cut and start over. But that was not to be.

~

THE SADDLING PADDOCK AT Belmont Park is gorgeous, with an ivy-covered gray stone grandstand as a backdrop. It simply exudes class. The horses strolled around under the trees and past neatly trimmed box hedges, gleaming as the sun shone on their shimmering coats. The crowd was huge and pressed tightly to the white iron railing, adding their vitality to the scene.

A.P. Indy was so late getting to the paddock, I was hoping he was going to be announced as a late scratch. As we continued to wait for his arrival, time seemed to stretch into an eternity. I had moved over and was chatting with Wayne Lukas when we heard a horse charging up the path.

A.P. Indy had finally arrived, making quite an entrance with a groom on either side, both of them hanging tightly to the two lip chains he was wearing. Barely under control, A.P. Indy was snorting and dancing, rearing up and looking for someone to kick. "Wow," I said to Wayne, "I'll have whatever he's had."

Later, as the field was loaded into the gate, again the crowd roared its approval when Casual Lies was announced. Then the field was under starter's orders, the crowd cheered and the horses were off. Casual Lies broke on the lead, with A.P. Indy right there with him. As they started around the first turn, Agincourt engaged us and A.P. Indy started to pull back off the fast pace, with Pine Bluff moving into third on the outside of him.

From where I stood in the grandstand I watched my

horse as he dueled for the lead from the time the gate opened until Agincourt ran out of gas on the turn for home. Pine Bluff stalked us and made his move as we rounded the turn, followed closely by A.P. Indy, who earlier had eased back even farther off the front runners. When the jockey riding A.P. Indy finally got the colt to the outside, where he liked to run, they came on strongly and ultimately won with ease.

My brave horse, who had dueled for the lead from the get-go, faltered badly when Pine Bluff and A.P. Indy engaged him. Casual Lies switched off his left lead onto his right lead exactly where he was supposed to at the head of the lane, but rather than accelerating, he started losing ground almost immediately. He finished the race in fifth, failing to beat Pine Bluff and losing out on the million-dollar bonus.

Obviously, something was wrong. Casual Lies always dug deep and found a little bit more. He had not folded like that since his second race. While I hustled back to the barn, I asked myself if he could have bled. A crowd of reporters was already gathering behind the barricade at the barn as Stanley was hosed off in preparation for his bath.

After the bath, I was looking closely for anything out of the ordinary. He wasn't coughing, so it was unlikely he had bled. He wasn't limping, and his tendons looked great. His knees and ankles had been cold and tight without medication of any kind that morning or for the previous two days.

I was looking down at Stanley's right ankle when he stopped for a drink of water. He stomped his foot at a fly, and right before my eyes, a gaping wound opened up on the hairline where the hoof meets the flesh. It wasn't a little hole either. You could have easily slipped your thumb into it when it gaped open, raw and bloody. I couldn't help flashing on an image in my memory of the sheet cake with the slice right through the legs.

I stopped Jim, and we immediately inspected the area. Almost one-fourth of Stanley's hoof wall had separated from its foundation. It must have come apart when he had changed from his left lead onto his right at the head of the lane. I have seen some nasty quarter cracks, but this one was humongous.

Quarter cracks are usually the result of an infection that happens between the hoof wall and the inner dermis, causing heat and pain. Normally, you can diagnose a quarter crack because the horse is lame with heat and a pounding pulse in the affected foot long before the crack bursts apart, but that hadn't been the case with Stanley. In a way I was relieved. I knew something had to be wrong for him to run so badly down the lane. All the reporters who were anxiously waiting saw us crouched down, looking at Stanley's hoof. I went over and gave them the news, explaining what had happened and how we would be removing the affected hoof wall the next day with the aid of a veterinarian. They wanted to know the time this surgery was going to take place.

Much to my surprise, they all showed up at the appointed time, ready to watch. Standing behind the barricades, they saw the vet deaden the area and Jim cut out the quarter crack under the supervision of our longtime friend and veterinarian from California, Herbert Wright. Ultimately Stanley lost a large section on the right side of his hoof, including a deep and significant portion of his frog.

I asked Herb how Stanley could not have been lame. He felt that because the crack had started out running from front to back, rather than up and down, it must have missed most of the major pain receptors until it grew big enough to cause the hoof wall to lose integrity and break away.

Stanley's hoof would stay packed with medicated bandages, changed twice daily, until all signs of fungus or infection were gone. At that point, he would be fitted with a handmade bar shoe that would protect the hoof and keep it from spreading while the affected area grew out. It would take months for the hoof to grow out completely.

Stanley was due for a vacation, and he was going to get it. The problem would be keeping him entertained sufficiently so that he wouldn't bounce around on his injured hoof because—bless him—he still wasn't limping.

~

THOUGH I DIDN'T CLICK my heels three times like Dorothy in her ruby slippers, our fairy tale had indeed come to an end, and it was time for all of us to return to California. Was I disappointed in Casual Lies' fifth-place finish in the Belmont Stakes? Into every good story comes a hard jolt of reality. I probably needed a good kick in my reality more than anyone.

Casual Lies overcame an allergic reaction to run second in the Kentucky Derby. He overcame a track unsuited to his running style to run third in the Preakness Stakes. But not even Casual Lies, my hero, could overcome the pain of a hidden quarter crack in his hoof, a crack that failed to surface before the long stretch run of the mile-and-a-half Belmont Stakes.

I would be a very callous person indeed if I said I was disappointed with my horse for yielding as he pounded down the stretch on his injured hoof. He succumbed to a pain that I would equate to having my toe ripped out with a pair of vise grips.

When the foot was opened up and we discovered the scope of the infection, we knew it had to have taken weeks, maybe even months, to develop to the extent it had. My horse had run through the entire Triple Crown with the same infirmity that had prevented A.P. Indy from running in either the Kentucky Derby or the Preakness, and yet Stanley had shown no symptoms, no heat, swelling along the hairline, pain—nothing. He had, however, shown the heart of a champion.

Casual Lies' pain tolerance was incredible. He'd never missed an oat or a carrot, he'd galloped with determination every time we'd taken him to the track, and he'd been unflaggingly cheerful and enthusiastic. Unfortunately, for him and us, if he hadn't been so tough, we could have discovered the problem sooner. We could have treated it before it had progressed so far, and we would have also been able to mitigate the damage.

Casual Lies took us on a Triple Crown odyssey beyond my wildest imagination. I had met so many wonderful people and had experienced a world of racing that only an elite few might consider normal.

I'd enjoyed the extended thrill of watching an ugly duckling nobody wanted turn into a world-class racehorse. Recognizing his incredible ability, I was encouraged to take on the big boys, who had all the advantages money could buy. Granted, we didn't always beat them, but we were close enough to cause anxiety.

I had the honor to inspire many of the "little people," like myself, to keep on trying in a very tough business that often appears to have the deck stacked against us. To find myself cast as a role model for innumerable young people who had dreams and aspirations for a future involving some aspect of the equine industry was humbling.

The media machine exposed me to fame, though fleeting, as it added life and color to a stressful and arduous time, while we were away from our home and out of our comfort zone.

The biggest factor, and the one that never changes, is the

difficulty in finding a young horse with enough talent and competitive spirit to compete in the Kentucky Derby. It borders on the impossible and has been compared to catching lightning in a bottle.

From the time I was a young girl reading about horses, the wheels were set in motion for me to be faced one day with the impossible. I spent hours scanning the library's bookshelves for horse stories, tales that sparked my imagination and made me dream about having my own horse to care for and ride.

Those dreams and the love I had for horses persisted into adulthood. They led me to follow paths rarely traveled by any woman, let alone one with my background. My refusal to give up on a dream eventually put me in the right spot, at the right time. Fate intervened when a nondescript, weedy brown yearling turned, looked into my eyes intently and captured my imagination.

The sparkling good humor reflected in those eyes only hinted at the possibilities to come. Over time, the tiny colt, whose charm captured everyone he ever came into contact with, grew into a magnificent stallion. The impossible had become the reality, and that reality, Stanley, had empowered me to embrace and believe in the dream.

My wonderful colt, with his marvelous personality, consistency and determination, became my friend and my inspiration. Mister Bright Eyes changed my life on so many levels. When I could have taken the money and sold Stanley, I chose the dream, the adventure and the memories of it all, particularly the ones that mean most to me now—his companionship. First, second or fifth, Stanley made both of us winners, and that will never be a casual lie.

Epilogue

Our return to Pleasanton coincided with the annual Alameda County Fair, and as we drove through the banner-covered stable gate we were completely unprepared for what amounted to a hero's welcome. As word spread of our arrival, from the guard on duty at the stable gate to the people rushing to greet us, smiling faces abounded, and tired after our cross-country flight, we were invigorated by the hearty reception.

We stopped frequently to speak with friends on the way to our barn, but eventually Stanley was unloaded from the trailer and led past a glorious display of yellow, orange and red roses that covered the trellis running along the outside of our shedrow. Stanley settled back into familiar surroundings to the sounds of cheerful voices chatting away. Fortunately the old barricades were still there—we certainly needed them over the next few days.

Honored as Grand Marshals of the 1992 Alameda County Fair parade, Jim and I rode in a convertible down Pleasanton's quaint and historic Main Street, lined with cheering people.

Homemade signs popped up everywhere: *We heart Casual Lies, Always a Stanley to Us, Get well Stanley, my foot hurts too.* I accepted a beautifully constructed bouquet of flowers and carrots one lady had pulled from her garden. The ribbon banner read: *We love Shelley Riley and Casual Lies.* It's easy to understand why I always return to Pleasanton—it's truly such a pleasant place to call home and where my heart wants to be.

Within days of our arrival, Lei Ling and her television crew showed up from New York to interview our friends and colleagues for Charles Kuralt's *On The Road* program. Cameras rolling, Jim was aboard Casual Lies as my wonderful colt paraded in front of the grandstand for a cheering crowd of hometown fans.

Meanwhile I was honored in the winner's circle by representatives from the California State Legislature who presented me with a resolution passed, signed and complete with the Great Seal of California affixed. This resolution commended Jim and me for our contribution to the recognition of horse racing in the State of California. There was also a resolution from the County of Alameda Board of Supervisors as well as plaques from the Alameda County Fair Association, the Pleasanton Chamber of Commerce, the Livermore Chamber of Commerce and the Alameda County Newspaper Groups. This was truly heady stuff, and as one woman's "I love you Shelley" rang out above the sound of the crowd, I was reminded that fame carried with it the responsibility of living up to expectations.

~

AFTER A WELL DESERVED vacation, giving the hoof time to heal, Casual Lies went back into training and started three more times in Southern California in the fall of 1992. He started in the Grade I Goodwood Handicap, the Grade III Volante Handicap, as well as the Grade III Lazaro S. Barrera Handicap, finishing fourth in each race. Although he was never beaten very far, he wasn't improving with each successive outing, and it was obvious that the Stanley who came out of these races was lacking his usual vigor.

Therefore I determined to give Casual Lies a much longer

period away from training and running. We chose to keep him with us at the racetrack, where we had control of his environment. He jogged most days with his buddy, the long-suffering Brownie. Stanley was in his own personal heaven, and it didn't take long for him to rediscover his enthusiasm. Once he was jumping out of his skin, it was time to put him back in training.

With seven months between starts, on June 26, 1993, Casual Lies stepped onto the sandy surface of Golden Gate Fields to contest the Golden Gate Budweiser Breeders' Cup Handicap, going one mile and one sixteenth on the dirt.

Despite some vocal criticism over my choice of races, Casual Lies won easily in 1:40:96, a shockingly fast time for the distance. Gary Boulanger, his latest jockey, confided he did it with ease and had plenty left in the tank.

Featured in the national news once again, and high on our glorious comeback, I started plotting our campaign, nominating Casual Lies to several nice races at Del Mar. Unfortunately fate had a nasty surprise in store for us, and in little more than a blink of an eye, I was reminded how fragile our horse could be. After a routine vaccination, Casual Lies came down with an injection-site abscess.

Never a fun thing to deal with, this abscess unfortunately went ballistic, and Stanley ended up in intensive care at the University of California at Davis Veterinary Hospital. I stayed with him twenty-four hours a day, snatching the occasional nap on a camp cot just outside his stall.

There were times when I held his head in my arms, sobbing as he shook in pain, his heart pounding unnaturally against the palms of my hands. At one point I confessed to Jim how fearful I was that we were going to lose him.

Once the multi-chambered abscess was isolated and drained, however, Casual Lies practically sighed in relief. For the first time since he had arrived at the hospital, Stanley slept peacefully right through to the next morning.

Although Stanley recovered quickly, he never seemed quite the same after coming so close to death. Obviously our plans for a summer campaign at Del Mar were off the table.

We were able to start Casual Lies twice more in the fall of 1993, in the Smile Handicap at Santa Anita and the Grade III Native Diver Handicap at Hollywood Park. Once again he ran fourth in both races, beaten by a fairly short margin.

Following a number of tremendously difficult decisions, Casual Lies was retired from racing in 1994. He had developed a very painful splint, a bony protrusion on the inside of the cannon bone just below the knee. Treatment would require either a risky surgery or an extensive period of time off, perhaps even a year or more.

At this point I realized the time he'd need to be off would place him at such a critical distance from his Triple Crown successes that it would be difficult to find a top notch breeding farm who was willing to take him on as a stallion. Stanley's standing at stud was now the major goal.

With a new crop of three-year-olds featured in the news media's coverage of the Triple Crown each year, many past runners are soon forgotten by the racing world. Even a horse that finishes second in the Kentucky Derby is soon forgotten if he doesn't run up a string of impressive wins in later outings.

However, Casual Lies' name recognition was still benefitting mightily from the Shelley Riley and Casual Lies news frenzy, which had garnered worldwide attention. This would not last forever—once a horse trained by a woman won the Kentucky Derby, our footnote in history would fade considerably. I had to let go of Stanley, and in all the painful thoughts about letting him go, my final thought was this: He had ensured my future, and it was time for me to ensure his.

The decision was made to place Casual Lies with Nelson and Sue Schick at their beautiful farm in New Zealand. At Nelson and Sue's Windsor Park Stud, which was as pretty as any farm I have ever seen in Kentucky, Stanley was housed in luxury, ridden every day and had his own private and lush green pasture.

Both Nelson and Sue were impressive in their accumulated experience in animal husbandry and the world of breeding championship Thoroughbreds. I knew that if Casual Lies had a chance to make it at stud and become a successful stallion, it would be with this knowledgeable couple.

Casual Lies stepped into his new career with alacrity and was soon getting many a nice foal for the New Zealand breeders. He sired the Group I stakes winners Coco Cobanna, So Casual and Maquire. The list of his winners goes on, and his influence continues.

Stanley finished out his life with Nelson and Sue on their 1,300-acre farm late in 2008. He was buried on the farm. They planted a tree next to his grave to honor his time there. It was so very hard to hear of his passing, and yet I comfort myself with knowing his happiness and welfare had been ensured for the rest of his days when I placed him in the caring hands of Nelson and Sue.

I sit here wiping tears off my eyeglasses with thoughts not only of Stanley, but of my amazingly talented husband as well. The best horseman I ever met, Jim Riley was diagnosed with a glioblastoma, a brain tumor, and passed away in January 2001, a few months following the diagnosis. He was only fifty-four years old, and his loss was a harsh one to deal with.

As for me, I moved to England for five years and spent

my time learning the UK culture and visiting the continent. Over the years I watched the New Year come in at Trafalgar Square in London, the Place de la Concorde in Paris and the Piazza del Popolo in Rome.

When I came back to the United States, I tried occupying my time writing for the Contra Costa Newspaper Group, taking on special feature articles and the occasional assignment in the real estate section. I became a very successful new car sales manager at a large BMW dealership, something that really had its moments.

For the last few years I have been trading in the stock market while fostering retired greyhounds. Rather quickly I ended fostering by adopting Nigel, a retired greyhound racer from Florida. Now the fastest Nigel ever runs is from the food bowl back to bed.

While endeavoring to fill out the pages of my Triple Crown diary into a memoir, I reconnected to that amazing time when my life revolved around Casual Lies in Louisville, Baltimore and New York. I found myself pulling the bricks out of the wall I had so carefully built in Europe to lock out the recollections that pained me.

I began embracing the memories rekindled by my notebooks, stacks of photographs and news stories, and what I discovered anew was something old and marvelous—the joy of owning, training and loving Casual Lies. What a wonderful thing I had denied myself for so many years.

Stanley wasn't just a horse to me—he was a life force I revered, a spirit with a personality that delighted and inspired me. Still, he *was* a horse, a good racehorse, and being part of his journey through the Triple Crown was an honor and a privilege that have become even more meaningful to me as the years pass.

I had taken a great chance in purchasing an unproven

yearling, of course, but the instant the auctioneer's hammer came down on that cold winter day in 1990, when a spunky and trusting young horse picked me to be his friend, I became a winner of much more than I had ever dreamed of achieving.

I am reminded how Stanley changed me. He made me a better person and, by his accomplishments, challenged me to believe in the impossible. Recognizing how the force of his nature influenced me so many years ago, I am left to wonder—could it happen again?

PHOTO

GALLERY

[Fig. 1] Casual Lies wins the Gr.III El Camino Real Stakes.

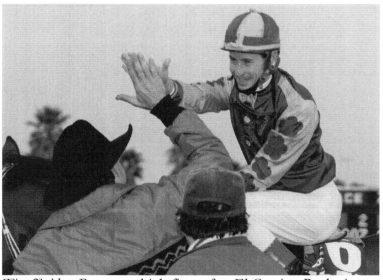

[Fig. 2] Alan Patterson high fives after El Camino Real win.

[Fig. 3] Press conference after the El Camino Real win.

[Fig. 4] Life is good for Classy at Two Ton Tony Farm.

[Fig. 5] Huge sense of relief after Sausalito Stakes win.

[Fig. 6] Those rascally parrots had just flown over at Santa Anita.

242

[Fig. 7] Negotiating the human gauntlet before the Kentucky Derby.

[Fig.8] Churchill Downs paddock, riders up for Kentucky Derby.

243

[Fig. 9] Oprah Winfrey came to see Stanley before the Preakness.

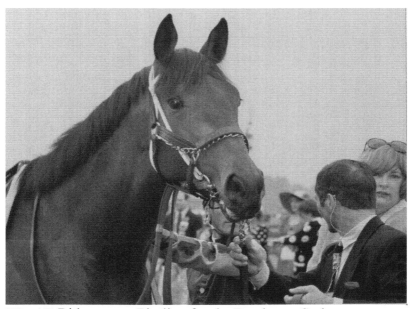

[Fig. 10] Riders up at Pimlico for the Preakness Stakes.

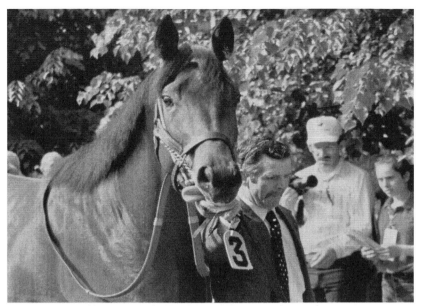

[Fig. 11] Stanley spotted another camera at the Belmont.

[Fig.12] Notice the crossed fingers during the Belmont Stakes.

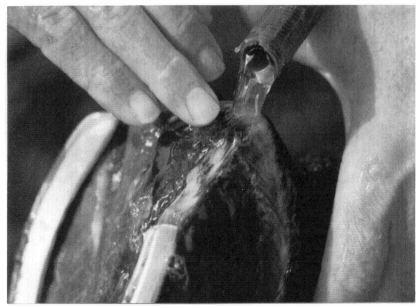

[Fig. 13] Stanley's hoof following the quarter crack surgery.

[Fig. 14] The Derby glasses nobody liked except me.

[Fig. 15] Jim, Stanley, Shelley outside Barn 3 at Belmont Park.

[Fig. 16] Reporters waiting in the rain at Pimlico.

[Fig. 17] Making them laugh at Belmont Press conference.

[Fig. 18] David & Lucille Fannin at Belmont Park.

Jim Riley   Helen Eisemann
1947-2001   1919-2000

Casual Lies
1989-2008

About the Author

SHELLEY RILEY lives in the San Francisco Bay Area with her rescued greyhound Nigel. She continues to support and encourage greyhound adoption groups, such as Walnut Creek's Golden State Greyhound Adoption. This group, along with a host of dedicated volunteers, has rescued, rehabilitated and placed over 1,300 greyhounds in loving homes.

For more information on Shelley, please visit
http://shelleyriley.com

Made in the USA
San Bernardino, CA
24 January 2014